HOW TO BUILD
AND MAINTAIN
RELATIONSHIPS
YOU TRUST

THE
TRUST
PRINCIPLE

John W. Fleck

For Information, Contact
Distributed by Skinny Brown Dog Media
SkinnyBrownDogMedia.com
Email Info@SkinnyBrownDogMedia.com

THE TRUST PRINCIPLE
How To Build and Maintain Relationships You Trust
By John Fleck
Email address: John@JWFleck.com
Website: JWFLECK.com

Library of Congress Cataloging in Publication Data
eBook 978-1-96-523514-0
Paperback 978-1-96-523511-9
Dust Jacket Cloth Cover Hardback 978-1-96-523512-6
Case Laminate 978-1-96-523513-3

CONTENTS

DEDICATION

To my daughters Kylie, Kennedy, and Kaylinn

You three are the heartbeat of my existence. Your laughter echoes
in the spaces between these pages, and your boundless love fuels
every word. Through your eyes, I've learned the true meaning
of joy, and in every second with you, I've found an unwavering
source of strength. This book is not just a dedication, but a
testament to the love that you've showered upon my life.

To my family, friends and mentors

In my journey, I have been fortunate to receive guidance, laughter, and
shared wisdom from each of you. Your belief in me has been a constant
wind beneath my wings. This book captures the essence of camaraderie,
showcasing the shared obstacles and triumphs we hold dear. Thank
you for being my compass and companions on this incredible odyssey.

A huge thank you to Evelyn Hills for her dedication
to her craft and unwavering faith

And to my Best Friend Chewie. You're not my dog, you are my heart.

FOREWORD

THE EMPHASIS ON mutual respect and the unwavering resolve of John Fleck's life serves as a powerful backdrop for the subsequent exploration of personal experiences and life lessons of trusting, love, replication, and success. The recounting of his early years, marked by relentless bullying, adds a personal touch to the book. The metaphor of a moral compass, inherited from your parents, provides a poignant image of resilience and self-discovery amid adversity. The book skillfully connects personal struggles with universal truths, making the story relatable and inspiring. The call to return to enduring principles in the face of a changing world is a timely and resonant message. The invitation to weave the Trust Principle into all aspects of life, transcending the boundaries of business, adds a layer of universality to the narrative. John conveys the transformative power of trust in shaping a life of boundless potential. John blends storytelling and philosophy seamlessly. The narrative style is engaging, and the metaphors used effectively convey complex ideas with simplicity. The book successfully sets the stage for the exploration of the Trust Principle and its transformative potential it can have in our lives and in business.

Mike Mayhugh, Senior Pastor, Henderson First Methodist Church and Author of "Battle Ready: Recognizing and Engaging in Spiritual Warfare"

I am delighted to endorse John Fleck's debut book, "The Trust Principle". In this compelling exploration of leadership, John skillfully explores the intricacies of effective leadership, presenting a nuanced and insightful perspective that is as refreshing as it is illuminating. Throughout the pages of this thought-provoking work, John draws upon his wealth of professional experience to dissect the core elements that define exceptional leadership. The book not only serves as a guide for aspiring leaders, but also resonates with seasoned professionals seeking to refine their leadership approach. John's keen observations and practical advice create a narrative that is not just informative but also profoundly actionable. My sincere congratulations to my colleague on the successful creation of this insightful work. "Trust" is not only a testament to John's expertise, but also a valuable contribution to literature on leadership. I have no doubt that readers will find inspiration, guidance, and practical strategies that will positively shape their leadership journeys. A must-read for anyone committed to honing their leadership skills and making a lasting impact in their professional sphere. Derek LaHair, Organizational Leader, Sexual Abuse Advocate, and author of the TedX talk "Unlocking Freedom with Forgiveness"

Derek LaHair, Organizational Leader, Sexual Abuse survivor, advocate, and author of the TedX Talk "Unlocking Freedom with Forgiveness"

Articulate, enlightening, with a sprinkle of entertainment, John brings the readers an irrefutable awareness of the Trust Principle and its vital application and impact on not only organizational leadership but into our personal lives as well. A great read and a great resource. Glad to add this book to my coaching library toolbox.

SFC (Retired) Jay Goff Personal Life & Executive Leadership Coach JKG Consultants LLC

John has written a unique book that combines a deep, practical topic with high literary flair. This is not your average business book!

Scott Wozniak, CEO of Swoz Consulting and Author of Make Your Brand Legendary

In The Trust Principle, you'll learn from reading, reflecting, and implementing John's five pillars of trust to enhance your success. You'll receive business, and life, direction and peace in a world saturated with confusion, mistrust, and angst.

Elizabeth McCormick, Motivational Speaker, Former Black Hawk Pilot at PilotSpeaker.com; Just named one of the Top 30 Motivational Speakers in the World

PROLOGUE

The Essence of Trust

IN THE GRAND scheme of life, trust is the unassuming piece of the puzzle that is necessary but is often lost in the hustle and bustle. It binds us together, creating a resilient network of relationships that withstand the tests of time and adversity. Trust is not merely a transaction; it's a currency of the heart, a force that propels individuals and businesses toward shared success.

In the everchanging landscape of today's world, trust often finds itself entangled in the complexities of modernity. As we navigate the digital age, where algorithms decipher our preferences and transactions occur with a click, the essence of trust can be overshadowed. Yet, at its core, trust has the simplest premise—when embraced in its purest form, it has the power to transform lives and businesses.

Simplification is the key to understanding and harnessing the true potential of trust. Imagine peeling away the layers of intricacy that surround our daily interactions, reducing them to their fundamental elements. What remains is trust, a timeless principle that forms genuine connections.

In business, trust is the currency that transcends profit margins and quarterly reports. It's the unseen force that compels customers to choose one brand over another, employees to give their best, and leaders to inspire with authenticity. Trust simplifies the complex dynamics of commerce, reminding us that success is not just measured in financial gains, but in the relationships that we build along the way.

Consider a handshake—an age-old gesture that embodies trust in its simplest form. In a single clasp, two individuals communicate volumes of intention, trust is the unassuming piece of the puzzle that is necessary but is often lost in the hustle and bustle. The beauty of the handshake lies in its simplicity; it cuts through the noise and gets to the heart of trust.

Simplicity in trust is about stripping away the unnecessary, allowing the essence of genuine connection to shine through. It's a return to the basics, a reminder that, amid the digital transformations and global complexities, the core principles of trust remain steadfast.

As we embark on this journey of exploration, let's unravel the layers that shroud trust in mystery and rediscover its simplicity. The TRUST Principle, distilled to its elemental pillars of trust, replication, utilization, service, and gratitude, serves as our guide. Together, we'll navigate the realms of personal and professional growth, understanding that simplicity not only clarifies but amplifies the transformative power of trust.

In the chapters that follow, we'll delve into each pillar, examining its nuances and uncovering the profound impact it has on our lives. But before we embark on this exploration, let us pause and reflect on the profound truth that simplicity reveals—the truth that trust, in its purest form, is the cornerstone of meaningful relationships and the catalyst for growth.

May we find clarity in simplicity, strength in connection, and inspiration in the ageless wisdom of the TRUST Principle. For in embracing trust, we open the door to a world where relationships flourish, businesses thrive, and the human spirit soars. Welcome to a journey of transformation—one where trust reigns supreme, and simplicity paves the way for a future built on the enduring foundation of shared principles.

Choose to trust the people in your life, and they will feel and act more trustworthy.

— William DeFoore

INTRODUCTION

The Power of Trust

"Trust is the glue of life. It's the most essential ingredient in effective communication. It's the foundational principle that holds all relationships." — Stephen R. Covey

IN THE SUMMER of 2005, I found myself standing at a crossroads. A major project at work was faltering, and the trust within our team was eroding. We were weeks behind schedule, tensions were high, and morale was at an all-time low. I remember looking around the conference room at the faces of my colleagues, sensing their frustration and uncertainty. It was at that moment I realized the missing piece trust.

I decided to take a leap of faith. I called a team meeting, not to discuss the project, but to have an honest conversation about our fears, frustrations, and expectations. I encouraged everyone to speak openly, assured that there would be no judgment. To my surprise, the atmosphere began to shift. As we shared our vulnerabilities, a sense of camaraderie emerged. We started to see each other as allies rather than adversaries. That day marked a turning point. By rebuilding trust, we were able to collaborate more effectively, meet our deadlines, and even exceed our original goals.

This experience taught me a valuable lesson trust is not just a nice to have; it is the cornerstone of any successful relationship, whether in business or in life. Without trust, communication breaks down, conflicts arise, and progress stalls. With trust, there is open dialogue, mutual respect, and a collective drive toward common goal.

The Importance of Trust

Trust is the foundation upon which all meaningful relationships are built. It is the invisible thread that connects individuals, teams, and organizations, enabling them to function cohesively and achieve remarkable outcomes. According to a study by Paul J. Zak, professor at Claremont Graduate University, high trust organizations experience significantly higher productivity, energy, and employee engagement compared to low trust organizations. In personal relationships, trust fosters deeper connections, enhances emotional intimacy, and creates a safe space for open communication.

In today's fast paced and often impersonal world, trust is more crucial than ever. We are constantly bombarded with information, much of which is conflicting or unreliable. In such an environment, trust acts as a stabilizing force, helping us navigate complexities and make informed decisions. A survey by the Edelman Trust Barometer found that nearly 70% of consumers consider trust to be one of the most important factors when purchasing from a brand. This underscores the vital role trust plays not just in personal interactions but also in economic and business contexts.

Research has shown that trust impacts every aspect of our lives. In the workplace, trust between employees and management leads to higher job satisfaction, lower turnover rates, and increased innovation. Teams that trust each other are more likely to collaborate effectively, share knowledge freely, and support one another through challenges. In personal relationships, trust reduces anxiety and stress, enabling individuals to be more open, honest, and supportive.

Introducing the TRUST Principles

To help you build and maintain trust in every aspect of your life, I have developed a framework known as the TRUST Principles. This framework is designed to provide practical strategies and insights that you can apply immediately. Here's a brief overview of each principle

- **Train** The foundational element for building competence and confidence. Training is about continuous learning, skill development, and personal growth. It's the first step in establishing a reliable foundation for yourself and others.

- Replication Learning from success by replicating effective strategies and behaviors. This ensures consistent and reliable outcomes. By identifying what works and duplicating those methods, we can achieve continuous improvement and avoid common pitfalls.
- Utilization Maximizing strengths by harnessing the unique talents and resources of individuals and teams. This involves recognizing and leveraging each person's skills to enhance overall performance and productivity.
- Service Supporting the growth and wellbeing of others, fostering a culture of mutual respect and collaboration. Service oriented leadership creates environments where people feel valued and motivated to contribute their best.
- Thankfulness Expressing gratitude regularly to build morale, reinforce positive behavior, and strengthen bonds. Gratitude fosters a positive atmosphere and encourages ongoing trust and cooperation.

In this book, you will learn how to integrate these principles into your daily life, transforming your relationships and achieving sustainable success. Whether you are a business leader, a team member, or someone looking to enhance personal relationships, the TRUST Principles will provide you with the tools you need to build a foundation of trust.

Here's what you can expect in the chapters ahead:

Chapter 1: Trust – The Foundation of Authentic Relationships

Welcome to the heart of it all! In this chapter, we're going to dive deep into what trust really means and why it's the bedrock of every meaningful relationship. We'll explore the psychology behind trust and discover how it forms those strong, lasting connections that make both personal and professional life flourish.

Chapter 2: Train - Building Skills and Knowledge

Get ready to roll up your sleeves! This chapter is all about the importance of training. We'll uncover the secrets to effective training methods and see how building skills and knowledge creates a trust-worthy and competent environment. Let's gear up to become masters of our craft.

Chapter 3: Replication - Learning from Success

Why reinvent the wheel when we can learn from success? In this chapter, we'll dig into how to replicate successful strategies to achieve consistent results. I'll share practical tips on identifying best practices and applying them effectively, ensuring we're always on the path to excellence.

Chapter 4: Utilization - Maximizing Strengths

It's time to shine a spotlight on our unique strengths! We'll uncover how to identify and leverage both our own talents and those of others. This chapter is a journey into creating a high-performing team where everyone's strengths are utilized to their fullest potential.

Chapter 5: Service - Supporting Growth and Well-being

Here's where we discover the true power of service. We'll delve into the importance of serving others and how it builds a supportive and thriving environment. By the end of this chapter, you'll see how service-oriented leadership can transform organizational culture and foster genuine growth and well-being.

Chapter 6: Thankfulness - Expressing Gratitude

Let's unlock the magic of gratitude together. This chapter explores the profound impact of thankfulness on our relationships. We'll dive into the psychological and emotional benefits of gratitude and find practical ways to weave it into our daily lives, enriching every interaction.

Chapter 7: The TRUST Principle in Action

Now it's time to put everything into practice. We'll look at real-world steps for integrating the TRUST principles into our everyday lives. This chapter is packed with actionable insights and tools to help you consistently and effectively live out these principles.

Chapter 8: Overcoming Challenges to Trust

Every journey has its obstacles, and we're going to tackle them head-on. We'll explore common barriers to trust and discover strategies to overcome them. This chapter will arm you with solutions to rebuild and maintain trust, no matter the challenges you face.

Chapter 9: Embracing Simplicity – Reinvigorating the Trust Principle

Simplicity is the ultimate sophistication. We'll rediscover the power of simplicity in applying the TRUST principles. This chapter will show you how simplifying our approach can amplify the impact of each principle, creating a more effective and harmonious environment.

Chapter 10: Real-life Examples of the TRUST Principle

Time for some inspiration! We'll explore detailed case studies of individuals and organizations that have successfully implemented these principles. These real-world examples will showcase the transformative power of the TRUST principles, providing us with powerful lessons and motivation.

Chapter 11: The Enduring Legacy of the Trust Principle

As we wrap up our journey, we'll summarize the key takeaways and inspire you to start building trust today. This conclusion will reinforce the importance of trust and encourage you to apply what you've learned to achieve lasting success. Let's make trust the legacy we leave behind.

By the end of this book, you'll have a comprehensive understanding of how to build and maintain trust in both your personal and professional life. Together, we'll embark on this transformative journey, discovering how trust can truly change your world and lead you to sustainable success. Let's get started!

Choose to trust the people in your life, and they will feel and act more trustworthy.

– William DeFoore

CHAPTER 1

TRUST

THE FOUNDATION OF AUTHENTIC RELATIONSHIPS

IMAGINE A SMALL West Virginia town in the heart of the 1970s, a place where every penny counted, and survival often felt like a daily battle. Yet, within these humble hills, a remarkable tapestry of joy and tranquility was woven—a tapestry that seems to have grown frayed and distant in the hustle and bustle of today's world.

As I delve into the recesses of my memory, I'm transported to a time when my neighbors were the pillars of unwavering resolve. They worked tirelessly; their hands calloused by the hard-earned dollars they scraped together. Despite their struggles, they blessed everyone they met with a priceless gift—a gift wrapped in respect and kindness. To them, treating people right was not contingent upon their financial woes; it was a nonnegotiable tenet of their character.

In our tightknit community, the very essence of neighborly living thrived. Here, everyone knew each other's names, and in the golden light of dawn or the cool embrace of twilight, they kept watchful eyes on one another's children. Laughter echoed through the streets, and the aroma of shared cookouts filled the air. It wasn't just about being neighborly—it was a closeknit community built on genuine connection.

1

My life's journey, much like yours, hasn't been a constant walk in the park. In my early years, I bore the weight of relentless bullying, a chapter of my life etched in the confines of my memories, leaving indelible marks on my life. Yet, in spite of this, I unearthed a treasure of profound importance—the boundless strength found in unwavering adherence to one's values and integrity.

Amid the tempest of bullying, I clung tenaciously to the moral compass my parents had gifted me. Holding onto my true self, even when the world conspired to crush me, became my guiding star. This trial engraved in me a firm belief that our internal values and principles are like unwavering lighthouses, illuminating the darkest nights and guiding us through life's most turbulent waters.

Today, as I watch the ever-transforming landscape of our world, I can't help but notice the fading echoes of laughter and the distant whispers of forgotten values. It is the yearning for a return to these enduring principles that fuels my passion to share the wisdom within this book with you.

While this book undoubtedly finds its roots in the fertile soil of business, its essence knows no boundaries, stretching far beyond the confines of office walls. It serves as an unbarred invitation to weave the Trust Principle into every intricate thread of your existence. As we set sail on this shared odyssey, take a moment to appreciate how the art of simplification can unlock unimaginable possibilities.

Just as a skilled artisan weaves threads into a masterpiece, you can weave trust into the fabric of your life, business, and spiritual growth, crafting a masterpiece of boundless potential. Let the principles contained within these pages be the chisel to carve away the unnecessary, unveiling the Magnus Opus that is your life.

Historical Perspectives on Trust

Throughout history, trust has been a cornerstone of societal development. In ancient societies, trust was essential for trade and governance. Merchants relied on trust to conduct business across vast distances, and rulers depended on trust to maintain order and loyalty. In many cultural traditions, trust is deeply ingrained in social norms and practices. For instance, in some indigenous cultures, trust is built through communal living and shared responsibilities, creating a strong sense of community and mutual support.

In ancient Greece, the concept of "philia," or brotherly love, was central to social cohesion. This form of trust was not just about emotional connection but also about mutual respect and loyalty. Similarly, in medieval Europe, the feudal system was heavily reliant on trust between lords and vassals, where mutual obligations and loyalty were paramount. These historical perspectives highlight how trust has always been a fundamental element in building and maintaining relationships.

Scientific Studies on Trust

Recent research in neuroscience and psychology provides valuable insights into the mechanisms of trust. Studies have shown that oxytocin, a hormone released during positive social interactions, plays a key role in trust formation. This "trust hormone" enhances bonding and social cohesion, making it easier for individuals to build and maintain trust. Psychological research also highlights the stages of trust development, from initial trust based on first impressions to deeper, established trust through consistent and reliable behavior.

One notable study conducted by researchers at the University of Zurich found that participants who received a dose of oxytocin were more likely to exhibit trusting behavior in economic transactions. This finding suggests that oxytocin not only facilitates social bonding but also promotes behaviors that reinforce trust in relationships. Another study from the University of California, Berkeley, revealed that expressions of gratitude significantly increased levels of trust and cooperation among participants.

Applying these findings in everyday life can significantly enhance our relationships. Simple actions like expressing gratitude, being transparent, and showing empathy can increase oxytocin levels, strengthening the bonds of trust. Understanding the stages of trust development can help us navigate relationships more effectively, recognizing that trust builds over time through consistent and trustworthy actions.

The Psychology of Trust

Building trust is a complex process that involves consistency, transparency, and vulnerability. At its core, trust is about predictability—knowing that someone will act in a way that aligns with our expectations. This predictability is built through repeated interactions where individuals demonstrate reliability and integrity.

From a psychological perspective, trust is deeply rooted in our brain chemistry. The hormone oxytocin, often referred to as the "trust hormone," plays a crucial role in forming and maintaining trust. Oxytocin is released in response to social bonding activities such as physical touch, positive social interactions, and expressions of gratitude. This chemical reinforcement helps solidify the bonds of trust between individuals.

Reflection Questions

1. Think of a time when you placed your trust in someone. What factors contributed to your decision to trust them initially?
2. Have you ever experienced a situation where your trust was broken? What were the consequences, and how did it impact your relationship with the person involved

Trust development can be seen as a staged process:

1. **Initial Trust:** This is the tentative trust we extend based on first impressions or the reputation of the other party. It is fragile and can be easily shattered if early interactions do not meet expectations. For example, consider a new employee joining a team. Their initial trust in the company and colleagues is based on the hiring process and initial interactions. If they encounter dishonesty or unprofessional behavior early on, this trust can quickly erode.
2. **Established Trust:** As interactions continue, trust becomes more solidified based on consistent and reliable behavior. This stage involves deeper interactions and a greater sense of security. For instance, a manager who consistently supports their

team, provides clear communication, and demonstrates fairness will establish trust over time.

3. **Reinforced Trust:** Over time, as trust is continuously validated, it becomes deeply ingrained and resilient to challenges. This is the highest level of trust, where both parties feel a strong, mutual commitment. An example of reinforced trust can be seen in longterm business partnerships where both parties have consistently met their commitments and supported each other through challenges.

One of the most transformative moments in my career unfolded during a high-stake project at work. As the deadline loomed and tensions mounted, trust within the team began to fray. The atmosphere grew thick with unspoken fears and mounting frustrations. Recognizing the need to address these underlying issues, I decided to take a bold step. I called a team meeting, inviting everyone to lay their cards on the table and openly discuss their concerns, anxieties, and expectations.

The room was charged with a mix of apprehension and hope as we embarked on this honest conversation. Voices that had been silent began to speak, revealing the vulnerabilities and aspirations that had been simmering beneath the surface. This candid exchange acted as a catharsis, breaking down barriers and forging a renewed sense of unity.

This pivotal moment became a turning point. As we confronted our challenges head-on, we rebuilt the trust that had been eroded. The team emerged stronger, more cohesive, and ultimately more successful than we had imagined possible. This experience underscored for me the profound power of trust in fostering effective collaboration and driving us toward achieving our goals.

Another example comes from a case study involving a tech company that struggled with internal trust issues. The leadership team decided to implement transparent communication strategies, regular teambuilding activities, and a recognition program to rebuild trust. Within a year, employee engagement and productivity significantly improved, demonstrating the tangible benefits of a trust centric approach.

Consider the story of Horizon Enterprises, a company that has thrived by embedding trust into its core values. Johnathan Reyes, the visionary founder, shared his journey on the TED stage, captivating the audience with stories of delegating challenging responsibilities to his team. This trust empowered his employees to innovate and explore unconventional solutions, leading to remarkable success. By recognizing strengths and empowering team members, Horizon Enterprises transformed its organizational culture and achieved sustained growth.

Reflection Questions

1. Recall a moment in your personal or professional life when you had to rebuild trust. What steps did you take, and what was the outcome?
2. Can you identify a leader or mentor in your life who exemplifies trustworthiness? What behaviors and actions make them stand out?

Types of Trust

Interpersonal Trust: This is the trust we have in individuals, such as friends, family members, and colleagues. It is built through direct interactions and personal experiences. Interpersonal trust forms the basis of our most intimate relationships, where honesty, loyalty, and mutual respect are paramount. For example, the trust between lifelong friends who have shared experiences, supported each other through challenges, and maintained consistent communication.

Organizational Trust: This type of trust exists within and towards organizations. It encompasses trust in leadership, the organization's values, and its commitment to stakeholders. Organizational trust is crucial for employee engagement and customer loyalty. Companies that prioritize transparency, ethical behavior, and employee wellbeing foster a culture of trust that drives performance and innovation. Consider the trust employees have in companies like Patagonia, which emphasizes environmental responsibility and ethical practices, leading to high levels of employee and customer loyalty.

Societal Trust: This is the trust we have in institutions and societal structures, such as government, legal systems, and public services. Societal trust influences our sense of security and community wellbeing. High levels of societal trust contribute to social cohesion, economic stability, and public confidence in institutions. An example of societal trust can be seen in countries with low corruption levels and strong legal systems, where citizens feel secure and trust in public institutions.

Reflection Questions

1. In your current relationships, whether personal or professional, which type of trust (interpersonal, organizational, societal) do you value the most and why?
2. Reflect on an organization you are part of or interact with. How would you rate the level of trust within this organization? What factors influence this trust level?

Intersections of Trust

Different types of trust are interconnected and can influence each other. For example, high levels of interpersonal trust within a team can enhance organizational trust, leading to a more cohesive and productive work environment. Conversely, a breach of trust in one area can ripple through other domains, undermining overall trust levels.

Consider a scenario where a company's leadership is caught in a scandal. This breach of organizational trust can erode interpersonal trust among employees, reduce customer trust, and even impact societal trust if the company is a significant community presence. Understanding these intersections helps in comprehensively addressing trust issues and fostering a culture of trust across various domains.

The dual nature of the TRUST Principle finds its clearest embodiment in the Replicate pillar. A leader replicates trust in their team members' abilities, and, in turn, team members mirror that trust in their leader's decisions. This symbiotic replication cultivates an environment where innovation blooms, where individuals feel empowered to contribute their unique perspectives without fear of reprimand.

The Utilize pillar exemplifies mutual respect, much like a conductor orchestrating a symphony. Just as each instrument gets its moment to shine, each team member's strengths are recognized, valued, and put to use. This respect isn't a one-way street; it flows in both directions.

Team members respect the leader's guidance, and leaders respect the individuality and potential of each team member.

Service and gratitude complete this reciprocal exchange. A client is not merely served by a business; they are the very reason for its existence. In return, the client receives topnotch service and conveys their gratitude through loyalty. This mutually beneficial service solidifies trust, nurturing a relationship that withstands the test of time.

In the intricate interplay of this two way street, a vital element must occupy a central place—mutual respect. Just as trust forms the bedrock of the TRUST Principle, mutual respect stands as the cornerstone upon which trust is built. When respect is absent, the bridge of trust crumbles, and the harmonious duet descends into a discordant solo.

Reflection Questions

1. Think about a time when a breach of trust in one area of your life affected other areas. How did you address it, and what did you learn from the experience?
2. How can you contribute to building a culture of trust in your workplace or community? What specific actions can you take?

Stephen M.R. Covey, in his book "The Speed of Trust," emphasizes that trust is a key driver of success in any relationship. He states, "Trust is the one thing that changes everything. It's the key to accelerated progress, improved results, and lasting relationships."

Brené Brown, a renowned researcher on vulnerability and trust, highlights the importance of vulnerability in building trust. She asserts, "Vulnerability is the birthplace of love, belonging, joy, courage, empathy, and creativity. It is the source of hope, empathy, accountability, and authenticity."

In the business realm, Paul J. Zak's research underscores the economic benefits of trust. He found that employees in high trust organizations are more productive, have higher job satisfaction, and exhibit greater loyalty to their employers.

These expert insights reinforce the central theme of trust's critical role in personal and professional success. Covey's emphasis on trust as a transformative element highlights its universal importance. Brown's focus on vulnerability shows how embracing authenticity can deepen trust. Zak's research provides a clear link between trust and tangible business outcomes, demonstrating that trust isn't just a nice to have but a vital component of organizational health.

Practical Strategies for Building Trust

Building and maintaining trust requires deliberate effort and consistent action. Here are some practical strategies:

1. Be Transparent: Openness and honesty in communication foster trust. Share information freely and be upfront about challenges and uncertainties. Transparency involves not just sharing positive news but also discussing setbacks and failures openly. For example, a company facing a financial crisis that openly communicates the situation and the steps being taken to address it can maintain employee trust.
2. Keep Promises: Reliability is a cornerstone of trust. Ensure you follow through on commitments and meet expectations consistently. This means not overpromising and underdelivering. Consistently meeting deadlines and fulfilling promises builds a reputation for dependability.
3. Show Vulnerability: Admitting mistakes and showing vulnerability can strengthen trust. It demonstrates authenticity and fosters deeper connections. Leaders who admit their mistakes and take responsibility for their actions create a culture of openness and trust.
4. Practice Active Listening: Pay full attention to others when they speak. Acknowledge their perspectives and respond thoughtfully. Active listening involves not just hearing words but understanding the emotions and intentions behind them. This practice shows respect and validation.
5. Express Gratitude: Regularly show appreciation for others' contributions. Gratitude reinforces positive behavior and strengthens relationships. Simple acts of gratitude, like saying thank you or recognizing someone's effort, can have a significant impact on building trust.

6. Build Consistency: Consistent behavior over time builds predictability and reliability, which are essential for trust. Consistency in actions, decisions, and behavior reinforces trust. For instance, a manager who consistently supports their team fosters a predictable and reliable work environment.

7. Encourage Collaboration: Create opportunities for teamwork and mutual support. Collaborative environments foster trust through shared goals and experiences. Encouraging team projects and collaborative problem-solving strengthens bonds and trust among team members.

8. Provide Support: Offer help and support to others, demonstrating that you care about their wellbeing and success. Providing support means being there for others in times of need, offering help and resources, and showing genuine concern for their success.

Reflection Questions

1. Which of the practical strategies for building trust resonate most with you? Why do you think they are effective?

2. Identify one strategy from the list that you haven't focused on much. How can you incorporate this strategy into your daily interactions.

Trust is the foundation of authentic relationships, driving effective communication, collaboration, and success. By understanding the psychology of trust, recognizing its different forms, and implementing practical strategies to build and maintain it, we can foster stronger, more resilient relationships in all areas of our lives. As we move forward in this book, we will delve deeper into each of the TRUST principles, providing you with

The Legacy of TRUST

On the illustrious stage of TED, a figure of distinction takes their place, their commanding presence instantly captivating the audience's attention. With a warm, genuine smile, they embark on a narrative journey, drawing the audience into the heart of their remarkable story. This is Johnathan Reyes, the visionary founder of Horizon Enterprises, a company renowned not only for its remarkable success but also for the enduring values that have guided it since its very inception.

In a modest office space, Johnathan's story begins, fueled by the unwavering belief in the Trust Principle that permeates the atmosphere. Using eloquent anecdotes, he enthralls the audience as he recounts instances of delegating challenging responsibilities to his team members. The outcome was a remarkable surge of innovation, as their unwavering trust in one another became the driving force behind their exploration of unconventional solutions.

As the company expanded, so did its application of the Trust Principle's pillars. Johnathan masterfully guides the audience through their evolutionary journey, painting vivid portraits of replication in action. He passionately relates how their inaugural groundbreaking product was replicated across diverse markets, resulting in resounding and consistent success, solidifying the profound value of replicating tried and true strategies.

Yet, it was not only about products; it was about people. With fervor in his voice, Johnathan expounds on the art of utilization—recognizing strengths and empowering team members to shine. He weaves together tales of employees, given opportunities to showcase their talents, who not only transformed their roles but also redirected the course of the entire company.

And what about service? A hint of vulnerability tinges Johnathan's voice as he delves into the company's challenging moments. He shares how their steadfast commitment to serving their employees during tumultuous times fostered bonds of unwavering loyalty and resilience. The audience leans in, captivated by the authenticity of the transformative journey he unfolds.

Finally, gratitude. Johnathan's eyes gleam with a genuine appreciation for every individual who has been part of Horizon Enterprises. He narrates poignant instances of employees being acknowledged, not just for their work, but for their unwavering dedication and contributions to the very spirit of the company.

The room is electric with a renewed sense of purpose. Johnathan's narrative isn't just about business success; it's a testament to the profound power of the Trust Principle in transforming lives. As he draws his talk to a close, the audience bursts into thunderous applause, profoundly moved by the simplicity and universality of these principles. Johnathan's journey becomes a guiding light, reminding us that these principles are not novel. They are the timeless foundation that once fortified businesses, nurtured relationships, and built resilient communities. And although they may have momentarily been overshadowed, they remain as relevant and transformative as ever.

Chapter Reflection Questions

Congratulations on completing this chapter! Trust is the foundation of all meaningful relationships, and reflecting on what you've learned is an essential step towards integrating these principles into your daily life. To help you process and apply these concepts, I've provided a series of reflection questions.

Consider starting a "Trust Notebook" where you can jot down your thoughts, insights, and plans. This notebook will serve as a personal guide and record of your journey in building and maintaining trust. Use it to document your reflections, track your progress, and revisit your entries as you continue reading.

Take your time with these questions. They are designed to be thought-provoking and practical, helping you to deeply internalize the principles discussed and to apply them in your personal and professional life.

Personal Trust Development

- Think about a recent relationship where trust was initially fragile. What actions helped establish and reinforce trust in that relationship?
- Can you recall a situation where trust was broken? How did you respond, and what steps did you take to rebuild trust?

Types of Trust

- In your current personal and professional relationships, which type of trust (interpersonal, organizational, societal) do you find most challenging to maintain? Why?
- Identify an organization you trust deeply. What specific actions or behaviors have contributed to this trust?

Building and Maintaining Trust

- Reflect on a time when transparency played a crucial role in building trust. How did being open and honest impact the relationship?
- Think about a promise you kept recently. How did fulfilling this commitment strengthen your relationship with the other person?

Expert Insights

- Which expert insight resonated most with you—Covey's, Brown's, or Zak's? How can you apply this insight to improve trust in your personal or professional life?
- How does vulnerability influence your ability to build trust? Can you think of a time when showing vulnerability helped you connect more deeply with someone?

Practical Strategies

- Of the practical strategies listed (transparency, keeping promises, showing vulnerability, active listening, expressing gratitude, building consistency, encouraging collaboration, providing support), which do you find easiest to implement? Which do you find most challenging, and why?
- Choose one practical strategy that you haven't focused on much. Develop a plan to incorporate this strategy into your daily interactions over the next month. What specific actions will you take?

Intersections of Trust

- How do you see the different types of trust (interpersonal, organizational, societal) intersecting in your life? Provide an example where trust in one area influenced trust in another.
- Reflect on a time when a breach of trust in one area of your life affected other areas. What lessons did you learn from this experience?

Real-life Applications

- After reading about Johnathan Reyes and Horizon Enterprises, identify a similar real-life example from your own experience or observation. How did trust play a role in their success?
- How can you apply the lessons from Horizon Enterprises to your own life or organization? What steps can you take to replicate their approach to building and maintaining trust?
- By engaging with these questions, you'll not only deepen your understanding of trust but also create a personalized action plan to enhance trust in your relationships. Your "Trust Notebook" will be a valuable tool in this journey, providing a space for reflection and continuous growth.

Trust is the first step to love

– Munshi Premchand

CHAPTER 2

TRAIN

BUILDING A FOUNDATION FOR SUCCESS

IN A WORLD dominated by technological advances, data driven decision-making, and complex methodologies, there remains a fundamental element whose value is often underestimated: Trust. This essential yet often overlooked element acts as the invisible lifeline that underpins both business interactions and personal relationships, serving as the cornerstone of success. Trust is what binds teams together, fosters innovation, and creates environments where individuals can thrive. Without it, even the most sophisticated strategies and advanced technologies can falter.

Imagine a scenario in which every handshake, every agreement, and every collaborative effort is underscored by an unspoken assurance that each party will act with integrity, honor commitments, and support each other's endeavors. This unspoken assurance is the essence of trust. In a rapidly evolving world where change is the only constant, trust becomes the bedrock upon which sustainable success is built. As we navigate through this chapter, we will delve into the profound significance of trust, exploring its multifaceted nature and understanding its pivotal role in shaping our professional and personal lives. We will uncover how trust acts as a catalyst for growth, innovation, and deeper connections, setting the stage for a more harmonious and successful existence.

Importance of Training for Trust Building:

Training serves as the bedrock of developing trust and achieving success in both personal and professional settings. Effective training methodologies can significantly enhance one's ability to build and maintain trust, leading to more robust and meaningful relationships. In this chapter, we will explore various training techniques that foster trust and provide detailed examples of their implementation and outcomes.

Training for Personal Development

Training for personal development is not merely about acquiring new skills but also about fostering trust in oneself and others. By investing time in personal growth, individuals can enhance their ability to build and maintain trust in various relationships. This section will discuss how different training methodologies can be employed to develop trust building skills, leading to stronger personal connections and a more fulfilling life.

Mindfulness: Practicing mindfulness helps individuals become more aware of their thoughts and emotions, allowing them to respond to situations with clarity and calmness. This self-awareness fosters trust in oneself and enhances one's ability to interact with others empathetically.

Mindfulness involves paying attention to the present moment without judgment. By focusing on the here and now, individuals can develop a deeper understanding of their internal states and reactions. This heightened awareness allows them to manage their emotions more effectively, reducing impulsive responses and fostering a sense of inner peace. When people practice mindfulness, they become more attuned to their feelings and thoughts, which helps them respond to situations with greater clarity and calmness. This self-awareness not only enhances their own wellbeing but also improves their interactions with others.

Consider Jane, a project manager at a tech company. She often found herself overwhelmed by the fast-paced nature of her job, leading to frequent stress and strained relationships with her team. After attending a mindfulness workshop, Jane began practicing mindfulness meditation for 10 minutes every morning. Over time, she noticed a significant reduction in her stress levels and an improvement in her ability to handle challenging situations. Her newfound sense of calmness and clarity allowed her to communicate more effectively with her team, fostering a more collaborative and trusting work environment.

Practical Steps:

1. Daily Meditation: Set aside 1015 minutes each day for mindfulness meditation. Focus on your breath and observe your thoughts and emotions without judgment.
2. Mindful Breathing: Practice mindful breathing exercises throughout the day, especially during stressful situations, to maintain a sense of calm and clarity.
3. Body Scan: Perform a body scan meditation to become aware of physical sensations and release tension.

Emotional Intelligence: Developing emotional intelligence involves understanding and managing one's emotions and recognizing and influencing the emotions of others. This skill is crucial for building trust in personal relationships.

Emotional intelligence (EI) is the ability to recognize, understand, and manage our own emotions while also being able to recognize, understand, and influence the emotions of others. High EI helps individuals navigate social complexities, build stronger relationships, and make informed decisions. By developing emotional intelligence, individuals can communicate more effectively, resolve conflicts amicably, and foster an environment of trust and mutual respect.

Consider Alex, a team leader who struggled with giving constructive feedback to his team members. He often came across as harsh and unapproachable, which led to decreased morale and trust within the team. After attending an emotional intelligence training program, Alex learned how to manage his emotions better and approach feedback with empathy and understanding. He began to recognize the emotional states of his team members and tailor his communication accordingly. This shift in approach helped Alex build stronger, more trusting relationships with his team, leading to improved performance and collaboration.

Practical Steps:

1. Self-Awareness: Reflect on your emotions and understand how they influence your thoughts and behavior. Keep a journal to track your emotional responses and identify patterns.
2. Self-Regulation: Practice techniques to manage your emotions, such as deep breathing, mindfulness, and positive self-talk. Avoid impulsive reactions by taking a moment to pause and reflect before responding.
3. Empathy: Develop empathy by actively listening to others and trying to understand their perspectives. Show genuine concern for their feelings and validate their emotions.
4. Social Skills: Enhance your social skills by practicing effective communication, conflict resolution, and teamwork. Focus on building positive relationships through trust and mutual respect.

Active Listening: Active listening involves fully concentrating, understanding, and responding thoughtfully to what others are saying. This practice shows respect and validation, reinforcing trust.

Active listening is a communication technique that requires the listener to fully engage with the speaker, understand their message, and respond thoughtfully. It involves paying attention to verbal and non-verbal cues, asking clarifying questions, and providing feedback. Active listening demonstrates respect and validation, making the speaker feel heard and valued. This practice strengthens trust and fosters deeper connections in both personal and professional relationships.

Consider Maria, a customer service representative who often dealt with frustrated customers. Initially, Maria would interrupt customers and offer solutions before fully understanding their concerns, which led to dissatisfaction and complaints. After receiving training in active listening, Maria began to approach each interaction with a focus on understanding the customer's perspective. She listened attentively, asked clarifying questions, and acknowledged the customer's feelings before offering solutions. This shift in approach resulted in higher customer satisfaction and trust in the company's commitment to addressing their needs.

Practical Steps:

1. Focus Attention: Eliminate distractions and give your full attention to the speaker. Make eye contact, nod, and use verbal affirmations to show that you are engaged.
2. Reflect and Paraphrase: Summarize what the speaker has said to ensure understanding and show that you are actively listening. Use phrases like "What I hear you saying is..." or "It sounds like you're feeling..."
3. Ask Open-ended Questions: Encourage the speaker to share more by asking open-ended questions that require more than a yes or no answer. This shows genuine interest in their perspective.
4. Provide Feedback: Offer thoughtful feedback and responses that demonstrate you have understood the speaker's message. Avoid interrupting or dismissing their concerns.

By incorporating these specific techniques for personal development, individuals can build a strong foundation of trust in their personal and professional lives. These practices not only enhance self-awareness and emotional intelligence but also foster deeper, more meaningful connections with others.

Organizational Training

In the business world, structured training programs are essential for fostering trust within organizations. By equipping employees with the skills, they need to succeed and creating an environment of continuous learning, organizations can build a culture of trust that drives performance and innovation.

Case Study: Trust Building Workshops

A company that implemented trust building workshops to address internal conflicts and improve team dynamics. The workshops included activities focused on teambuilding exercises, transparent communication, and conflict resolution strategies. As a result, employees began to understand each other's perspectives better, leading to improved collaboration and a more cohesive work environment. The increased trust among team members translated into higher productivity and job satisfaction.

Types of Training Programs:

1. Leadership Training: Developing leaders who can inspire trust through their actions and decisions is crucial for organizational success. Leadership training programs focus on ethical decision-making, transparent communication, and empathetic leadership.
2. Team Building Exercises: These activities help build trust among team members by fostering collaboration, understanding, and mutual respect. Effective teambuilding exercises create a sense of camaraderie and shared purpose.
3. Conflict Resolution Training: Equipping employees with conflict resolution skills ensures that disputes are handled constructively, maintaining trust and harmony within the organization.

Reflection Questions:

1. Think of a time when training significantly improved your trust in someone or something. What made the training effective?
2. Reflect on a training program at work. How did it enhance trust among team members?

Reflection Questions for Chapter:

Personal Trust Development:

1. Think about a time when trust in your abilities was a key factor in your success. What actions or decisions reinforced that trust?

2. Recall an instance where a lack of trust hindered your success. How did you address the situation, and what were the outcomes?

Types of Trust:

1. Which type of trust (interpersonal, organizational, societal) do you believe is most crucial for achieving success in your field? Why?
2. Identify a successful organization you admire. What trust building practices do they employ that contribute to their success?

Building and Maintaining Trust:

1. Reflect on a project or task where maintaining transparency was critical to its success. How did open communication impact the outcome?
2. Think about a commitment you fulfilled that significantly contributed to a successful outcome. How did this strengthen trust with your team or stakeholders?

Expert Insights:

1. Which insight on trust from experts like Covey, Brown, or Zak do you find most applicable to achieving success? How can you implement this in your professional life?
2. How does demonstrating vulnerability contribute to your success? Share an example where being vulnerable led to a successful collaboration or project.

Practical Strategies:

1. Of the strategies for building trust, which one has been most effective in your path to success? Which remains a challenge, and why?

2. Select a practical strategy you haven't prioritized. Create a plan to integrate this strategy into your professional life over the next month. What specific actions will you take?

Intersections of Trust:

1. How do different types of trust (interpersonal, organizational, societal) intersect in your professional life? Provide an example where trust in one area bolstered success in another.
2. Reflect on a situation where a breach of trust in your professional life affected your success. What did you learn from this experience?

Real-life Applications:

1. After reading about Johnathan Reyes and Horizon Enterprises, think of a similar success story from your experience. How did trust play a crucial role?
2. How can you apply the trust building lessons from Horizon Enterprises to your own career or organization? What steps can you take to emulate their success?

By engaging with these questions, you'll not only deepen your understanding of trust but also create a personalized action plan to enhance trust in your relationships. Your "Trust Notebook" will be a valuable tool in this journey, providing a space for reflection and continuous growth.

Replicate

I built the business exactly the way my mother built and ran her family. I wanted a replication of the big, happy family I grew up in. I wanted people having fun.

– Barbara Corcoran

CHAPTER 3

REPLICATE

LEARNING FROM SUCCESS

IN AN ERA where innovation and groundbreaking ideas reign supreme, there is an enduring lesson to be gleaned from history: success has a distinct trail of footprints. It's within the realm of replicating these well-trodden paths, the proven and successful approaches, that we find the essence of the Replicate pillar within the Trust Principle. This chapter unfurls the profound potency of replication, delving deep into its application across both the business landscape and personal relationships. It serves as a poignant reminder that building upon what has already been proven to work stands as a steadfast route to attaining enduring success.

Replicating Successful Approaches in Business

Visualize a scenario within business where a team achieves nothing short of remarkable success through the diligent implementation of a specific strategy. This could take the form of a product launch that mesmerizes the market or the seamless integration of an efficient workflow, ushering in a paradigm shift in productivity. It is precisely in such moments that the Replicate pillar comes into sharp focus, calling upon us to not merely acknowledge these victorious approaches but to consciously replicate them in other domains.

Replicating these successful strategies instills a culture in businesses that values consistency and efficiency. Rather than embarking on the arduous task of reinventing the wheel with each new challenge, teams can, instead, draw upon the wealth of tried-and-true methods at their disposal. This pragmatic approach not only conserves time and valuable resources but also ensures that the invaluable lessons harvested from previous triumphs continue to illuminate the path for future endeavors.

What's more, the act of replication serves as a powerful force in fortifying the bonds of collaboration. As team members bear witness to the unequivocal positive outcomes born from these successful strategies, they are inspired to rally behind these proven approaches. A palpable sense of trust in the team's collective capabilities burgeons, as each member comes to recognize that their individual contributions hold profound value and are instrumental in shaping the larger picture.

Case Study: Scaling Sales Strategy Across Regions

Consider a business that has successfully scaled its operations by replicating a successful sales strategy across different regions. This company initially developed a robust sales approach in its home market, which included comprehensive customer analysis, targeted marketing campaigns, and an effective sales team structure. After witnessing significant growth and positive customer feedback, the company decided to replicate this strategy in other regions.

By meticulously documenting the sales process, training new sales teams, and monitoring progress through key performance indicators (KPIs), the company achieved consistent results across all new markets. The replication of this proven strategy not only expanded the company's market presence but also reinforced a culture of success and reliability within the organization.

Principles of Replication in Business:

1. Documentation and Standardization:
    *   Clearly document successful processes and procedures.
    *   Standardize these processes to ensure consistency across all areas of the business.
2. Training and Development:
    *   Provide thorough training for employees to ensure they understand and can implement the replicated strategies.
    *   Continuous development and support to adapt and improve the strategies over time.
3. Monitoring and Evaluation:
    *   Regularly monitor the implementation of replicated strategies.
    *   Use metrics and KPIs to evaluate performance and make necessary adjustments.

Steps to Replicate Business Success:

1. Identify successful strategies.
2. Document and standardize processes.
3. Train employees to follow the standardized processes.
4. Monitor and adjust as necessary to ensure consistency and quality.

Reflection Questions

1. Think of a successful strategy you have implemented in your workplace. How can this strategy be replicated in other areas or projects?
2. Reflect on a time when a lack of replication led to wasted resources or missed opportunities. What could have been done differently?

Replicating Positive Experiences in Personal Relationships

The principle of replicating successful strategies applies to both businesses and personal relationships, as they both rely on the reproduction of positive experiences. Reflect upon a treasured memory shared with a loved one, be it an impromptu road trip or a heart-to-heart conversation that brought you closer. The Replicate pillar inspires us to be purposeful in our endeavors to recreate such moments.

Replicating positive experiences within personal relationships serves as the nurturing force for emotional bonds. It grants individuals the opportunity to relive instances of joy and profound connection, reinforcing the positive emotions that have come to be intertwined with these cherished experiences. This practice, in essence, operates as a touching reminder of the shared history and the profound depth that defines the relationship.

Moreover, the scope of replication within personal relationships extends far beyond the confines of experiences; it encompasses attitudes and behaviors as well. When we replicate a thoughtful gesture or respond empathetically, we effectively communicate our care and deep appreciation for the other person. This bolsters the bedrock of trust that underpins relationships, creating a self-sustaining cycle of reciprocity that further strengthens the emotional connection.

Replicating Success in Fitness Training

Consider John, who successfully improved his fitness levels through a structured training regimen. Inspired by his achievements, he decided to replicate the same disciplined approach to improve his career performance. John identified key behaviors that contributed to his fitness success, such as setting clear goals, maintaining a consistent schedule, and tracking his progress. He applied these principles to his professional life by setting specific career objectives, creating a detailed action plan, and regularly reviewing his progress.

As a result, John not only achieved his career goals but also developed stronger relationships with his colleagues. His commitment to replicating successful behaviors fostered a sense of trust and reliability, making him a valuable and respected team member.

Principles of Personal Replication:

1. Self-Reflection:
   - Regularly reflect on past successes and identify key behaviors and strategies that contributed to those achievements.
2. Goal Setting:
   - Set clear, achievable goals based on past successes.
   - Create a detailed action plan to guide your efforts.
3. Consistency:
   - Maintain consistency in your efforts to replicate successful behaviors.
   - Regularly review and adjust your strategies as needed.

Steps to Replicate Personal Success:

1. Identify successful behaviors or strategies.
2. Reflect on and document the processes that led to success.
3. Set clear, achievable goals.
4. Maintain consistency and monitor progress.
5. Adjust strategies as needed to stay on track.

Reflection Questions

1. Think about a memorable experience you have shared with a loved one. How can you recreate similar moments to strengthen your bond?
2. Reflect on a time when you replicated a positive behavior or gesture in a relationship. How did this impact the relationship?

Learning from Failures: A Path to Improvement

Replication isn't a concept confined to successes alone; it extends its reach to encompass the terrain of failures as well. The lessons learned from failed endeavors often possess a distinct and deep significance. In the realm of business, the candid acknowledgment and meticulous examination of failures can yield insights of paramount significance, serving as guiding stars for future decisions. A climate of transparency about these failures within a team begets trust and fosters openness, for members come to realize that the emphasis here is placed on learning and growth, rather than a futile hunt for scapegoats.

In the sphere of personal relationships, the practice of recognizing and learning from one's mistakes acts as a robust adhesive, strengthening the bonds between individuals. Offering heartfelt apologies and seeking to make amends serves as a testament to one's humility and an unwavering commitment to the wellbeing of the relationship. Replicating this attitude of growth and accountability contributes to cultivating a culture defined by mutual respect and unwavering trust.

Overcoming a Business Setback

A tech startup faced a significant setback when a major product launch failed due to technical issues. Instead of pointing fingers, the leadership team decided to conduct a thorough postmortem analysis to understand what went wrong. They identified key areas for improvement, such as better-quality control and more rigorous testing protocols. By openly acknowledging their mistakes and implementing these improvements, the company successfully launched their next product, regaining customer trust and achieving strong market performance.

Principles of Learning from Failures:

1. Transparency:
   - Foster a culture of transparency where failures are openly acknowledged and analyzed.
   - Encourage team members to share their experiences and insights.

2. Continuous Improvement:
   - Use the lessons learned from failures to drive continuous improvement.
   - Implement changes and monitor progress to ensure long-term success.

Steps to Learn from Failures:

1. Acknowledge and analyze failures.
2. Identify key lessons and areas for improvement.
3. Implement changes and monitor progress.
4. Foster a culture of continuous learning and improvement.

Reflection Questions

1. Think of a failure or setback you have experienced in your professional or personal life. What lessons did you learn, and how can you apply these lessons to future endeavors?
2. Reflect on a time when acknowledging and learning from a mistake strengthened your relationship with someone. How did this experience affect your trust and connection?

Breaking Down the Mold: Chick-fil-A- Crafting a Consistent Culinary Experience

The story of Chick-fil-A, the illustrious fast-food chain, serves as a living testament to the Replicate pillar within the Trust Principle. Chick-fil-A's journey isn't simply about serving delicious chicken. It's about replicating an experience that resonates harmoniously across their expansive network, epitomizing the very essence of the Replicate principle.

Chick-fil-A's Method for Replication

1. Uniformity Beyond Boundaries:
   - Chick-fil-A's narrative transcends mere expansion; it's a tale of duplicating excellence. Whether nestled in the heart of bustling cities or gracing the serene landscapes of quiet towns, Chick-fil-A consistently replicates an unwavering experience. The warmth of service, the delectability of their menu, and the vibrant ambiance remain unwavering, underscoring their unwavering commitment to the art of replication.

2. Meticulous Consistency:
   - Every Chick-fil-A establishment adheres to an intricately crafted blueprint. From the sincere and cordial "My Pleasure" response to the personalized touch in customer interaction, no detail is left unattended. This unwavering dedication to detail ensures a replicated experience, engendering a sense of familiarity and comfort no matter which Chick-fil-A one chooses to visit

3. The Art of Training:
   - The triumph of Chick-fil-A's replication story rests upon a robust training regimen. Their employees undergo comprehensive preparation that extends beyond the realm of mere tasks; it is a deep immersion in the brand's ethos and culture. This rigorous training guarantees a replicated standard of service and excellence, uninhibited by geographical location.

4. A Recipe That Transcends Cuisine:
   - Chick-fil-A's replication doesn't halt at the boundaries of their menu; it's deeply woven into the very fabric of their corporate identity. The spirit of courtesy and community involvement is likewise replicated. Their unswerving commitment to giving back, as seen in initiatives like employee scholarships and community gatherings, reverberates harmoniously across all their establishments.

5. Expansion with Precision:
   - Chick-fil-A's strategy for expansion mirrors the core of the Replicate principle. It's not about hasty and unchecked proliferation; it's about a deliberate and strategic approach, one that extends their reach while unwaveringly replicating their core values and commitment to quality. This measured and thoughtful approach ensures that they maintain their commitment to excellence as they extend their influence.

Chick-fil-A's success story illustrates the power of replication in maintaining quality and consistency across locations. By adhering to a meticulous blueprint and rigorous training, they create a reliable and trusted brand experience.

Applying Replication's Lesson

Chick-fil-A's triumph serves as a profound ode to the art of replication, aligning seamlessly with the principles of the Trust Principle. It underscores the idea that successful methods deserve to be replicated, but it's not a mere act of imitation; it's about adopting functional strategies and executing them with unwavering consistency.

The lesson we can draw from Chick-fil-A's story is that this replication principle is not confined to the business realm alone. It's equally relevant in our personal and professional lives. This involves acknowledging and replicating the strategies that have proven to be effective, resulting in consistent and reliable outcomes. Chick-fil-A teaches us that replication is more than just copying; it's about creating a reproducible experience that customers, partners, or our loved ones can trust and rely on.

Reflection Questions

1. Identify a successful relationship where trust played a key role. What specific actions or behaviors can you replicate in other relationships?
2. Reflect on a time when replicating successful trust building actions led to improved outcomes in a different relationship.

Starbucks - Brewing Consistency and Trust Across the Globe

In the bustling heart of Seattle back in 1971, a modest coffee shop named Starbucks opened its doors. Initially, it was a single store dedicated to the sale of premium coffee beans and equipment. However, over the years, it has transformed into a global sensation. The key to Starbucks' remarkable success lies in their dedication to replicating not only their products but also the values that define their brand.

Starbucks did not simply replicate the process of brewing coffee; they replicated an unparalleled experience that customers could find across the globe. As Starbucks expanded, they meticulously adhered to their core principles: quality, community, and connection. The company realized that replicating their approach to creating a welcoming atmosphere and providing personalized customer interactions was just as vital as replicating the taste of their signature beverages.

With each new Starbucks location, their aim was to recreate the ambiance of the original store, where customers could savor more than just a cup of coffee. They could immerse themselves in a culture of comfort and conversation. This replication of ambiance nurtured trust, as customers knew they could walk into any Starbucks, anywhere, and discover a familiar sense of comfort and consistency.

Starbucks' commitment to replicating quality extended beyond their physical stores. They replicated their sourcing practices, ensuring that the coffee beans they used were of the highest quality and ethically sourced. This dedication to replicating their ethical standards not only earned the trust of customers but also forged strong relationships with coffee farmers around the world.

Starbucks' global success is rooted in their ability to replicate a consistent and trusted experience across locations. By adhering to core principles and ethical standards, they build a loyal customer base and establish themselves as a reliable brand.

The Replicate pillar of the Trust Principle underscores the importance of learning from both successes and failures. It highlights the power of building upon what works and acknowledging what doesn't. By consciously replicating successful strategies and positive experiences, we create a foundation of consistency and trust that can lead to enduring success.

As we journey through this book, let's embrace the wisdom that comes from past achievements and mistakes alike. Let's apply these lessons with intentionality, knowing that the path to lasting success often lies within the well-trodden footsteps of those who have come before us. By doing so, we honor the past, enrich the present, and pave the way for a future defined by trust and success.

Reflection Questions

1. Identify a successful relationship where trust played a key role. What specific actions or behaviors can you replicate in other relationships?
2. Reflect on a time when replicating successful trust building actions led to improved outcomes in a different relationship.

Types of Trust:

1. Which type of trust (interpersonal, organizational, societal) do you find easiest to replicate in new situations? Why?
2. Think of an organization that has consistently earned your trust. What replicable actions contribute to their trustworthiness?

Building and Maintaining Trust:

1. Describe a situation where transparency in a successful project helped build trust. How can you replicate this approach in future projects?
2. Recall a promise you kept that led to a successful outcome. How can you replicate this commitment keeping behavior in other areas?

Expert Insights:

1. Which expert insight on replicating trust building actions resonates most with you? How can you apply this to replicate success in your personal or professional life?
2. How does showing vulnerability help replicate success in building trust? Share an example where vulnerability led to a successful replication of trust building actions.

Practical Strategies:

1. Of the practical strategies for building trust, which have you successfully replicated in different contexts? Which remain challenging, and why?
2. Choose one practical strategy you haven't yet replicated effectively. Develop a plan to incorporate this strategy into your interactions over the next month. What specific actions will you take?

Intersections of Trust:

1. How do different types of trust (interpersonal, organizational, societal) intersect when replicating successful behaviors? Provide an example where trust in one area influenced replication in another.
2. Reflect on a time when a breach of trust in one area hindered your ability to replicate success. What lessons did you learn from this experience?

Real-Life Applications:

1. After reading about Johnathan Reyes and Horizon Enterprises, identify a similar situation in your experience. How did trust play a role in replicating success?
2. How can you apply the replication lessons from Horizon Enterprises to your own life or organization? What steps can you take to replicate their approach to building and maintaining trust?

Take a minute to sit with these questions, you'll not only deepen your understanding of trust but also create a personalized action plan to enhance trust in your relationships. Your "Trust Notebook" will be a valuable tool in this journey, providing a space for reflection and continuous growth.

Utilize

***The true test of anyone's worth as a living
creature is how much he can utilize what he has."***

– Anton LaVey

CHAPTER 4

UTILIZE

HARNESSING STRENGTHS

IN A WORLD that thrives on diversity and celebrates individuality, the Utilize pillar of the Trust Principle takes center stage, shedding light on the profound significance of identifying and harnessing the distinctive strengths of each person. This chapter delves deep into the art of utilization, unveiling its relevance within the realms of both business ventures and personal relationships. By embracing and amplifying the potential of every individual, we unravel a rich supply of capabilities that have the potential to propel us toward unprecedented levels of achievement.

Utilization is not just about recognizing someone's talents; it's about strategically placing those talents where they can have the most significant impact. Imagine an orchestra where the violinist is forced to play the trumpet. Even though the violinist might manage to produce some sound, it would be a far cry from the harmonious symphony that could be achieved if everyone played to their strengths. This analogy holds true in both professional settings and personal relationships. When individuals are placed in roles that align with their natural abilities, not only do they perform better, but they also find more satisfaction and fulfillment in their tasks.

In the business world, effective utilization means more than just delegating tasks based on skill sets. It involves creating an environment where employees feel valued and understood. When team members see that their unique talents are being used optimally, they are more likely to engage fully with their work, contributing to a more dynamic and innovative organizational culture. This goes beyond mere job satisfaction; it fosters a sense of belonging and loyalty, which are crucial for long-term success.

In personal relationships, utilization can transform the dynamics of how we interact with our loved ones. Recognizing and appreciating the strengths of friends and family members can lead to deeper, more meaningful connections. It's about seeing the unique qualities in those around us and encouraging them to shine. Whether it's acknowledging a friend's knack for planning the perfect trip or appreciating a family member's ability to listen without judgment, utilizing these strengths enhances the bond and trust within relationships.

Moreover, the concept of utilization is deeply intertwined with growth. When individuals are given the opportunity to use their strengths, they not only excel in their current roles but also develop new skills and capabilities. This continuous growth is beneficial for both the individual and the collective entity, whether it's a team, a family, or a community. It creates a ripple effect where the success and development of one person can inspire and uplift others around them.

As we explore the Utilize pillar in this chapter, we will look at various strategies and reallife examples that illustrate the power of effective utilization. From the structured environment of a thriving business to the intimate connections of personal relationships, we will uncover how recognizing and leveraging individual strengths can lead to extraordinary outcomes. The aim is to provide you with practical insights and tools that you can apply in your own life, helping you to build stronger, more resilient relationships and achieve greater success in all your endeavors.

Utilizing Strengths in Business

Businesses are like symphonies, with each member contributing their unique notes and talents to create a harmonious masterpiece. The Utilize pillar of the Trust Principle serves as the conductor, orchestrating this symphony by recognizing and leveraging individual strengths. Imagine a project team that resembles a diverse orchestra, where every member contributes their unique instrument—strategic thinking, creative design, and analytical prowess. The conductor's role is to allocate the right instruments to the right players, ensuring that the team performs at its peak.

This practice is more than just efficient; it's empowering. When team members are entrusted with roles that align with their strengths, it sends a powerful message that their unique talents are not only recognized but valued. This recognition boosts their confidence and ignites their motivation, making them more invested in the project's success.

For instance, consider a marketing team tasked with launching a new product. By assessing each team member's strengths, the team leader might assign the creative individual to design the marketing materials, the strategic thinker to develop the campaign plan, and the analytical expert to handle market research. This strategic utilization ensures that each aspect of the project benefits from the team's collective expertise, leading to a more cohesive and effective campaign.

Moreover, the Utilize pillar fosters a culture of inclusivity and collaboration. When employees see that their unique skills are being utilized and appreciated, they are more likely to feel a sense of belonging and commitment to the organization. This not only enhances individual performance but also strengthens the overall team dynamic, paving the way for sustained success.

Case Study: Strength Based Assessments:

A company that uses strength-based assessments to place employees in roles where they excel can see increased productivity and job satisfaction. For example, Gallup's StrengthsFinder tool helps identify employees' top strengths and align their roles accordingly. This alignment boosts engagement, reduces turnover, and fosters a culture of excellence.

Principles of Utilizing Strengths in Business:

1. Strengths Identification:
    *   Implement tools and assessments to identify individual strengths.
    *   Encourage employees to discover and understand their unique strengths.

2. Role Alignment:
    *   Align roles and responsibilities with individual strengths.
    *   Create opportunities for employees to use their strengths in their daily work.

3. Ongoing Development:
    *   Provide continuous development opportunities to enhance and leverage strengths.
    *   Offer training and resources to support strengths-based growth.

Reflection Questions:

1. Think of a successful strategy you have implemented in your workplace. How can this strategy be replicated in other areas or projects?
2. Reflect on a time when a lack of replication led to wasted resources or missed opportunities. What could have been done differently?

Utilizing Strengths in Personal Relationships

Much like businesses that thrive by tapping into the strengths of their team members, personal relationships bloom when individuals acknowledge and harness each other's distinctive qualities. Visualize a closely-knit circle of friends, each possessing a distinct talent—one excels at meticulously organizing events, while another is known for their ability to provide unwavering empathy and support. The Utilize pillar becomes a guiding light for friends, encouraging them to make the most of these unique qualities to elevate the dynamics of the group.

Utilizing these strengths within personal relationships goes beyond just creating a pleasant atmosphere; it fosters profound connections. When friends not only recognize but genuinely value each other's distinct contributions, it cultivates a profound sense of mutual support. Each person's strengths become like complementary instruments in an orchestra, each note enhancing the harmony of the group experience. It's the art of harnessing individual talents for the collective good, and in the realm of personal relationships, it strengthens the bonds that tie friends together.

Consider a family where each member has a unique role. The father might be the planner, organizing family trips and ensuring everything runs smoothly. The mother could be the nurturer, providing emotional support and maintaining harmony. The children might bring their creativity and energy to the family, planning fun activities and keeping the atmosphere lively. By recognizing and valuing these roles, the family can function more cohesively and supportively.

In friendships, the Utilize pillar encourages individuals to tap into their unique strengths to support and uplift each other. For example, if one friend is an excellent listener and another is great at giving practical advice, they can play to these strengths in times of need. This mutual support strengthens the friendship and ensures that each person feels valued and understood.

A Narrative About a Couple Improving Their Relationship:

Share a story about a couple who improved their relationship by focusing on and appreciating each other's strengths. For instance, a couple where one partner is good at planning and the other at cooking can split household tasks to play to their strengths, leading to a more harmonious relationship.

Principles of Utilizing Strengths in Personal Relationships:

1. Strengths Awareness:
    *   Encourage open conversations about individual strengths within relationships.

- Promote mutual understanding and appreciation of each other's strengths.
2. Strengths-Based Support:
   - Provide support and encouragement based on each other's strengths.
   - Collaborate on activities and projects that align with individual strengths.
3. Celebrating Strengths:
   - Celebrate achievements and milestones that highlight individual strengths.
   - Acknowledge and appreciate the contributions of each other's strengths in the relationship.

Reflection Questions:

1. Think about a memorable experience you have shared with a loved one. How can you recreate similar moments to strengthen your bond?
2. Reflect on a time when you replicated a positive behavior or gesture in a relationship. How did this impact the relationship?

Growth through Effective Utilization

The practice of effective utilization transcends immediate advantages; it serves as a catalyst for personal and professional growth. In the business realm, when individuals are provided opportunities to apply their strengths, they become avid learners. As they harness their unique talents, they accumulate knowledge and experiences that not only benefit their current roles but also propel their careers to new heights.

In the realm of personal relationships, the Utilize pillar becomes a nurturing force for personal growth. When friends and family members are encouraged to pursue their passions and interests, they embark on journeys of self-discovery and fulfillment. This sense of fulfillment extends its positive influence to their relationships, creating an atmosphere of support, encouragement, and shared joy.

Effective utilization plays a pivotal role in shaping well-rounded individuals. By recognizing existing strengths and fostering the acquisition of new skills, both businesses and personal relationships contribute to the holistic development of individuals. As a result, this holistic growth fosters a culture where mutual respect thrives, as individuals develop a deep appreciation for the diverse range of talents that every person brings to the table.

Case Study: Gallup's StrengthsFinder Implementation:

Detail how an organization implemented Gallup's StrengthsFinder, and the positive outcomes observed. Discuss the process, challenges, and lessons learned from this implementation.

Principles of Effective Utilization:

1. Strengths Identification:
    *   Use assessments and tools to identify individual strengths.
    *   Encourage self-awareness and exploration of unique talents.
2. Strengths Application:
    *   Align roles and responsibilities with strengths.
    *   Create opportunities for individuals to apply their strengths in meaningful ways.
3. Continuous Growth:
    *   Provide ongoing development opportunities to enhance strengths.
    *   Encourage a growth mindset and continuous learning.

Reflection Questions:

1. Think of a failure or setback you have experienced in your professional or personal life. What lessons did you learn, and how can you apply these lessons to future endeavors?

2. Reflect on a time when acknowledging and learning from a mistake strengthened your relationship with someone. How did this experience affect your trust and connection?

Aces in Places: The Chick-fil-A Lunch Rush

Visualize a bustling Chick-fil-A during its lunch rush—a constant stream of customers, the symphony of trays and cutlery, and a whirlwind of orders. In the midst of this orchestrated chaos, a strategy called the "Aces in Places" approach emerges, which is a perfect embodiment of the Utilize pillar of the Trust Principle.

Chick-fil-A's lunchtime frenzy isn't a haphazard affair; it's a precisely choreographed performance that magnifies the art of utilizing strengths. "Aces in Places" isn't just a catchy slogan; it's a guiding philosophy that strategically positions team members in roles that align with their unique talents, enhancing efficiency, elevating service, and nurturing trust.

Picture a team member, Susan, who possesses a rare ability to swiftly take orders, process payments with precision, and maintain a warm rapport with customers. Susan isn't randomly assigned; she's stationed at the front counter, where her talents shine the brightest. Here, she efficiently manages the deluge of orders, ensuring both accuracy and a delightful customer experience. Susan's utilization in this critical role amplifies overall team performance, reduces wait times, and stands as a vital pillar of Chick-fil-A's lunch rush strategy.

But the "Aces in Places" approach doesn't conclude at the front counter. In the kitchen, you find Mark, a master of culinary precision. Mark's utilization in the kitchen ensures orders are meticulously and expeditiously prepared, maintaining the high-quality standards that Chick-fil-Ais renowned for. Mark's role transcends mere cooking; it's about upholding the trust that customers place in Chick-fil-A's consistent taste and service.

The beauty of the "Aces in Places" strategy lies in its meticulous orchestration. Team members' strengths are assessed, acknowledged, and positioned in roles that align seamlessly with their talents. It's not about applying a one size fits all strategy: it's about recognizing the diversity of strengths within the team and harnessing them to their fullest potential.

The "Aces in Places" strategy during the lunch rush is more than just an operational tactic; it's a reflection of Chick-fil-A's unwavering commitment to its employees and customers. Through the strategic leveraging of individual strengths, Chick-fil-A has succeeded in establishing an environment where team members not only prosper but also achieve remarkable results. Service quality soars, and trust flourishes. Customers depart not only satisfied with their meal but also with an experience that resonates with the very essence of the Utilize pillar.

Beyond the confines of Chick-fil-A's lunchtime rush, the lessons of the Utilize pillar extend to every facet of life. Just like Chick-fil-A leverages its strengths during its peak hours, we can also utilize our natural talents to enhance our efficiency and effectiveness in all aspects of our lives, whether personal or professional. Through training, introspection, and a steadfast commitment to utilization, we can replicate the success of Chick-fil-A's "Aces in Places" strategy in our own lives, amplifying our potential and nurturing trust in every endeavor.

Principles of "Aces in Places":

1. Strengths Assessment:
    - Regularly assess and identify individual strengths.
    - Align roles and responsibilities with assessed strengths.

2. Strategic Positioning:
    - Position team members in roles that leverage their unique talents.
    - Ensure that strengths are utilized to maximize efficiency and service quality.

3. Continuous Improvement:
    - Provide training and development opportunities to enhance strengths.
    - Encourage a culture of continuous improvement and excellence.

Reflection Questions:

1. Think about a situation where you or someone else was placed in a role that did not align with their strengths. How did this impact the outcome?
2. Reflect on a time when you effectively utilized your strengths or those of your team. What were the results and what did you learn from this experience?

The Parable of the Talents: Maximizing Resources and Trust

In the Gospel of Matthew, Jesus imparts profound wisdom through the Parable of the Talents, a story that intricately illustrates the concept of utilization. This parable delves into the essence of utilizing one's resources and abilities through the narrative of three servants entrusted with varying amounts of money, referred to as talents, by their master.

Before departing on a journey, the master distributes talents to his servants, recognizing their individual abilities. He entrusts five talents to one, two talents to another, and one talent to the last servant. Upon his return, he summons the servants to render an account of their actions.

The servant bestowed with five talents had astutely utilized his resources, doubling his investment. Similarly, the one with two talents had multiplied his share. Their master recognized and praised both of them for their resourcefulness and the effective way in which they utilized their entrusted talents.

However, the servant who had received a single talent made a different choice. Instead of employing it, he buried it in the ground, motivated by fear of his master's expectations. When questioned about his inaction, he offered excuses rather than using the talent he had been given. The master's disappointment was not due to the smaller amount but the servant's failure to utilize the entrusted resources.

This biblical parable underscores the significance of effectively using one's abilities and resources. It serves as a reminder that each individual possesses unique strengths and gifts that should be maximized. The master's praise for the diligent servants who multiplied their talents mirrors the principle of utilization, encouraging us to recognize our own strengths and harness them for personal growth, as well as within the contexts of our relationships and endeavors.

The Parable of the Talents resonates beyond its biblical setting, transcending into our lives as a profound reminder that utilization isn't solely about personal gain. The primary objective is to show our gratitude for the trust that has been given to us by maximizing the resources that we have been provided. When we acknowledge and make good use of our abilities, we actively contribute to a world that fosters growth, innovation, and fulfillment, echoing the ageless wisdom that is embedded within this parable.

Principles from the Parable of the Talents:

1. Resource Identification:
   - Identify the resources and talents you have been entrusted with.
   - Recognize the unique strengths and abilities within yourself and others.
2. Effective Utilization:
   - Use your resources and talents to their fullest potential.
   - Maximize the impact of your strengths through strategic application.
3. Growth and Contribution:
   - Focus on growth and continuous improvement.
   - Contribute positively to your community and the world around you.

Reflection Questions:

1. Think of a time when you effectively utilized your strengths and resources. How did this impact your personal or professional life?
2. Reflect on a situation where you failed to utilize your strengths. What lessons did you learn, and how can you apply them to future endeavors?

The Utilize pillar of the Trust Principle emphasizes the importance of recognizing and harnessing individual strengths. By effectively utilizing these strengths, we can create environments that foster collaboration, growth, and success. Whether in business or personal relationships, the practice of utilization leads to deeper connections, increased efficiency, and a sense of fulfillment.

Utilization is not just about assigning tasks based on skill sets; it's about creating a culture where every individual feels valued and understood. In professional settings, this leads to more dynamic and innovative organizations. In personal relationships, it fosters deeper, more meaningful connections. The practice of effective utilization transcends immediate advantages and acts as a catalyst for continuous growth and holistic development.

As we continue to explore the Trust Principle, let us embrace the diverse talents and abilities within ourselves and those around us. By doing so, we can build stronger, more resilient relationships and achieve greater levels of success in all areas of our lives. The key is to understand, value, and strategically utilize the unique strengths each person brings to the table.

Chapter Reflection Questions:

Congratulations on completing this chapter! Reflecting on what you've learned is an essential step towards integrating these principles into your daily life. To help you process and apply these concepts, I've provided a series of reflection questions.

Take your time with these questions. They are designed to be thought-provoking and practical, helping you to deeply internalize the principles discussed and to apply them in your personal and professional life.

Personal Trust Development:

- Think about a relationship where trust in your strengths played a critical role. How did utilizing your strengths enhance the relationship?

- Recall a situation where recognizing and utilizing someone else's strengths helped build trust. How did this impact the outcome?

Types of Trust:

- Which type of trust (interpersonal, organizational, societal) do you find most important when harnessing strengths? Why?
- Identify an organization that effectively utilizes its strengths to build trust. What specific actions contribute to this?

Building and Maintaining Trust:

- Reflect on a time when transparency about your strengths and limitations helped build trust. How can you continue to utilize this approach?
- Think about a promise you kept by utilizing your strengths. How did fulfilling this commitment strengthen your relationship with others?

Expert Insights:

- Which expert insight on utilizing strengths to build trust resonates most with you? How can you apply this in your personal or professional life?
- How does showing vulnerability about your strengths and weaknesses help build trust? Share an example where this approach led to a positive outcome.

Practical Strategies:

- Of the practical strategies for building trust, which have you successfully used to harness your strengths? Which remain challenging, and why?

- Choose one practical strategy you haven't focused on much. Develop a plan to better utilize your strengths in your interactions over the next month. What specific actions will you take?

Intersections of Trust:

- How do different types of trust (interpersonal, organizational, societal) intersect when utilizing strengths? Provide an example where trust in one area influenced the effective use of strengths in another.
- Reflect on a time when a breach of trust affected your ability to utilize your strengths. What lessons did you learn from this experience?

Real-Life Applications:

- After reading about Johnathan Reyes and Horizon Enterprises, identify a similar situation from your experience. How did trust play a role in effectively utilizing strengths?
- How can you apply the lessons from Horizon Enterprises to your own life or organization? What steps can you take to better utilize strengths in building and maintaining trust?

Explore these questions to gain deeper insights into trust and develop a tailored strategy for strengthening trust in your relationships. Your "Trust Journal" will serve as a personal guide, offering a dedicated space for introspection and ongoing development.

By reflecting on these prompts, you'll:

1. Uncover your own trust patterns
2. Identify areas for improvement
3. Create actionable steps to build stronger, more trusting connections

Use this process as a springboard for open conversations and personal growth, ultimately fostering more authentic and resilient relationships.

Serve

The best was to find yourself is to lose your-self in the service of others."

– Mahatma Gandhi

CHAPTER 5

SERVE

SUPPORTING GROWTH AND WELLBEING

IN A WORLD where personal goals often take precedence, the Serve pillar of the Trust Principle stands out as a guiding light, reminding us of the deep significance of putting the needs of others first. This chapter delves into the artistry of service, unraveling its profound influence not only in the business realm but also within personal relationships. The Serve pillar, dedicated to creating a space where individuals feel genuinely supported and appreciated, transcends being a mere principle and instead becomes a cornerstone that cultivates an environment fostering both personal growth and collective wellbeing.

Service is more than an act; it is an embodiment of our commitment to the wellbeing of others. When we serve, we signal that we value and respect those around us. This selflessness builds a culture of trust and cooperation, creating a foundation for strong relationships and successful organizations. Whether in the boardroom or at home, the principle of service is timeless and universal, bridging the gap between personal aspirations and collective success.

Serving in Business

In the realm of business, serving team members transcends the fulfillment of immediate needs; it entails crafting an environment that nurtures their growth and wellbeing. Envision a scenario where leaders prioritize the requirements of their team, offering essential resources, guidance, and mentorship. The deliberate choice to allocate resources towards developing team members not only enhances their skills but also instills within them a strong drive to contribute their utmost to the organization.

A culture of service within a business fosters an environment where employees feel valued and supported. This support can take many forms—professional development opportunities, mental health resources, or simply a listening ear. When leaders show genuine concern for their employees' wellbeing, it encourages a reciprocal commitment from the team. This mutual dedication propels the organization toward collective achievements and fosters a profound sense of shared purpose.

Examples:

1. Mentorship Programs:

Imagine a tech company that implements a mentorship program to support new hires. This initiative not only helps newcomers navigate their roles but also builds a supportive network within the company. Mentorship encourages knowledge sharing and creates a sense of belonging, which are critical components of a thriving workplace. Employees who feel supported are more likely to be engaged, productive, and loyal, leading to reduced turnover and higher morale.

2. Professional Development:

Consider a company that prioritizes continuous learning and development for its employees through workshops, courses, and career advancement opportunities. Such initiatives not only enhance employees' skills but also show that the company is invested in their longterm success.

3. Health and Wellness Programs:

Providing comprehensive health and wellness programs, including mental health support, gym memberships, and flexible working hours. These programs demonstrate a commitment to the overall wellbeing of employees, fostering a healthier and more productive workforce.

Strategies for Implementation:

1. Employee Centric Programs:

Develop and implement programs that prioritize employee wellbeing, such as mental health support, flexible working hours, and professional development opportunities.

2. Customer Centric Initiatives:

Create initiatives that serve customers beyond basic transactional relationships, such as customer feedback loops, loyalty programs, and exceptional customer service.

3. Community Engagement:

Invest in community projects, encourage volunteerism among employees, and form partnerships with local organizations to address community needs.

Reflection Questions:

1. How do you currently support the growth and wellbeing of your team members or employees?
2. Reflect on a time when serving others in your professional life led to stronger relationships and increased trust.

Serving Friends and Family in Personal Relationships

Serving friends and family vividly reflects the Trust Principle's power to enrich lives on a personal level. This chapter intricately explores how serving friends and family becomes the lifeblood of nurturing enduring connections, grounded in the principles of trust, replication, utilization, service, and gratitude.

1.   Trust as the Foundation:

Trust lays the cornerstone of personal relationships. Demonstrating consistency, reliability, and openness builds a trust that fortifies the foundation of enduring bonds.

2.   Replicating Acts of Love:

Replicating acts of love and support fosters harmony across personal relationships. Successful gestures, such as attentive listening and genuine appreciation, can be replicated to cultivate a culture of mutual understanding and care.

3.   Utilizing Each Other's Strengths:

Acknowledging and utilizing each other's strengths enhances personal relationships. Recognizing and respecting individual talents not only fortifies your connections but also fosters mutual growth.

4.   Serving Wholeheartedly:

Serving friends and family means being there wholeheartedly. Offering unwavering support, dedicating time, and sharing resources in times of need underscore your commitment to their wellbeing.

5.   Gratitude in Everyday Moments:

Expressing gratitude in everyday interactions amplifies personal relationships. Recognizing the unique value each individual brings to your life fosters mutual respect and deepens connections.

Examples:

1.   Daily Acts of Service:

Simple gestures like preparing a meal for a loved one, helping a friend move, or offering a shoulder to cry on during tough times can significantly strengthen bonds. These actions demonstrate a commitment to the wellbeing of those you care about, reinforcing trust and deepening emotional connections.

2.   Long-term Commitments:

Engage in long-term service commitments, like volunteering for local charities, mentoring, or organizing community events.

3. Service Based Communication:

Foster open communication about needs and ways to serve each other better in personal relationships.

Reflection Questions:

1. Think about a time when serving others in your personal life led to a stronger relationship. What specific actions did you take, and what was the outcome?
2. How can you incorporate more acts of service into your daily interactions with loved ones?

Creating a Culture of Support

The idea of service extends far beyond individual and isolated actions. In the business world, a culture of support can lead to increased employee satisfaction, reduced turnover, and heightened creativity. Individuals feel valued, and this sense of value translates into higher engagement and productivity.

Creating a culture of support in the workplace involves more than just offering resources; it requires a shift in mindset. Leaders must prioritize the wellbeing of their employees, recognizing that a happy and healthy workforce is a productive one. This can be achieved through policies that promote work life balance, such as flexible working hours and remote work options, as well as programs that support mental and physical health.

Strategies for Implementation:

1. In the Workplace:
- Implement policies that promote work life balance, such as flexible working hours and remote work options.
- Establish programs that support mental and physical health, like wellness programs and access to counseling services.

2. In Personal Relationships:
- Schedule regular check-ins with friends and family to discuss needs and concerns.
- Foster open communication and create a platform for mutual support and understanding.

Reflection Questions:

1. How can you contribute to creating a culture of support in your workplace or personal life?
2. What changes can you make to ensure the needs of those around you are acknowledged and met?

Patagonia Serving People and Planet

Nestled amid the majestic peaks of the Sierra Nevada Mountains, Patagonia transcends the conventional definition of a clothing company; it stands as a living testament to the transformative power of service to both humanity and the planet. Since its inception in 1973, Patagonia's visionary founder, Yvon Chouinard, envisioned a business that went beyond creating outdoor apparel—it sought to make a positive impact on the environment and the lives of its employees.

Detailed Analysis:

1. Environmental Sustainability:

Patagonia's commitment to environmental sustainability is evident in their use of organic materials and donations to environmental causes. Their decision to donate 100% of their Black Friday sales to grassroots environmental organizations highlights their dedication to service over profit.

2. Employee Well Being:

Patagonia's employee centric policies include flexible work hours, onsite childcare, and support for activism. This approach isn't merely about creating a more favorable workplace; it's a profound commitment to serving the diverse needs of their employees and cultivating a culture rooted in mutual support.

3.   Customer Trust:

Patagonia's service-oriented philosophy has built trust and loyalty among its customers. People aren't merely purchasing products; they're investing in a company that authentically cares about making a positive impact. This bond of trust between the company and its customers stands as a driving force behind Patagonia's success, underscoring the profound impact of prioritizing service in the realm of business.

Reflection Questions:

1.   What aspects of Patagonia's approach to service resonate with you?
2.   How can you incorporate similar principles of service into your personal or professional life?

As we explore the Serve pillar, let's remember that supporting others isn't just a gesture; it's a powerful force that nurtures growth and wellbeing. By prioritizing the needs of team members, friends, and family, we contribute to a culture where individuals thrive and relationships flourish. Through the use of real-life examples and practical insights, we will continuously peel back the layers of the Serve pillar. This process will reinforce the idea that dedicating ourselves to service can act as a catalyst for significant changes, not only in our professional lives but also in our personal journeys.

Service is a commitment to making the world a better place, one act at a time. Whether in a business context or within personal relationships, serving others builds a foundation of trust and mutual respect. It creates environments where people feel valued, supported, and empowered to reach their full potential. The Serve pillar of the Trust Principle is not just about doing good; it's about being good and creating a legacy of positive impact.

Final Reflection Questions:

1. Reflect on a recent experience where you served others. How did it impact both you and the recipients of your service?
2. What steps can you take to make service a more integral part of your daily life?

Thank

Make it a habit to tell people thank you. To express your appreciation, sincerely and without the expectation of anything in return. Truly appreciate those around you, and you'll soon find many others around you. Truly appreciate life, and you'll find that you have more of it

– Ralph Marston

CHAPTER 6

THANK

EXPRESSING GRATITUDE

IN A SOCIETY that thrives on speed and constant activity, where the overwhelming chaos often obscures the finer points, the pillar of Thank in the Trust Principle arises as a gentle yet compelling influence, quietly underscoring the deep significance of expressing gratitude. This chapter embarks on a nuanced exploration of thankfulness, peeling back its layers to reveal its impact not only within the confines of the business arena but also within personal relationships. Through the perspective of gratitude, we discern the profound impact of recognizing the efforts of others, illustrating how nurturing a culture of appreciation enhances the Thank element as a foundational cornerstone for uplifting morale, fortifying bonds, and establishing trust.

At the heart of the Thank pillar lies the art of recognition—a deliberate act of acknowledging and appreciating the efforts, talents, and contributions of those who shape our professional and personal landscapes. Imagine a workplace within the everchanging world of business, where expressions of gratitude are not just polite gestures but essential elements of everyday interactions. Leaders who openly acknowledge the dedication of their teams, team members who express gratitude for collaborative efforts—such a culture becomes a catalyst for cultivating a positive, appreciative ethos. The environment we find ourselves in allows the Thank pillar to prosper, creating a sense of camaraderie, nurturing motivation, and laying a solid groundwork for collective achievements.

The transformative effects of gratitude extend seamlessly beyond the office walls. In the intimacy of personal relationships, the Thank pillar manifests as a genuine appreciation for the unique qualities, gestures, and support offered by friends and family. Picture a scenario where individuals, amidst the ebb and flow of daily life, routinely express gratitude for the small yet significant acts of kindness, understanding, or unwavering support. This practice becomes the adhesive binding relationships, creating a resilient foundation built on mutual respect, empathy, and unwavering understanding.

The pillar of gratitude not only boosts morale and strengthens bonds but also acts as a powerful trigger for trust. In the dynamic world of business, leaders who authentically express gratitude sow the seeds of trust and loyalty. Team members, feeling recognized and valued, respond with heightened commitment, propelling the organization toward collective success. Similarly, within personal relationships, the act of expressing gratitude is an essential component. It can be compared to threads intricately woven into the fabric of trust, which further strengthens emotional connections and creates an environment where individuals feel seen, valued, and empathetically understood.

Let us embark on the chapters devoted to the exploration of gratitude with a keen awareness of how its impact can endure. The intentional and authentic practice of gratitude transcends the immediate moment and becomes a cornerstone for lasting transformation. Through reallife examples and practical insights, we will continue to unveil the layers of the Thank pillar, revealing how a simple expression of thanks possesses the transformative power to not only brighten someone's day but also to reshape the landscape of our professional and personal spheres.

Expressing Gratitude for Business Success

In the dynamic landscape of business, where accomplishments are frequently marked and swiftly succeeded by new aspirations, the deliberate practice of expressing gratitude emerges as a transformative force.

Envision a situation where a leader takes a break to convey genuine gratitude to team members for their unwavering devotion and diligent contributions. This seemingly straightforward action surpasses mere appreciation—it communicates a profound understanding that individual contributions are not only valued but essential, uplifting morale and fostering a collective sense of belonging.

The impact of gratitude within the business sphere extends beyond individual acknowledgment; it sets off a ripple effect that resonates through team dynamics. As leaders and team members alike genuinely appreciate each other's contributions, a culture of mutual respect blossoms. This environment, characterized by the sincere expression of gratitude, becomes the fertile ground for open communication, collaborative synergy, and a shared commitment to the journey of success. In this nuanced space, each gesture of thanks becomes a building block, reinforcing the bonds that propel the team toward collective achievements.

At TechMission, a software development firm, weekly "Gratitude Meetings" have become a cornerstone of company culture. During these gatherings, employees publicly thank colleagues for their contributions. This simple yet powerful practice has yielded impressive results: boosted morale, increased job satisfaction, and enhanced team cohesion. By fostering a culture of appreciation, TechMission demonstrates that in the fast paced tech world, taking time to express gratitude can significantly impact workplace dynamics and overall success.

Is this length more suitable for your needs? I can adjust further if necessary.

Reflection Questions:

1. How often do you take the time to express gratitude to your team members?
2. What are some ways you can incorporate more expressions of gratitude into your daily business interactions?

Gratitude and Appreciation in Personal Relationships

Just as in the realm of business, gratitude assumes a pivotal role within personal relationships. Visualize a group of friends who regularly express their appreciation for the presence and support they provide to one another. The act of expressing gratitude goes beyond just exchanging pleasantries; it holds deeper meaning.

Within families, the act of expressing gratitude becomes a potent force shaping emotional intimacy. When family members consistently take the time to acknowledge and appreciate each other's efforts, it goes beyond mere recognition—it becomes a powerful affirmation of the inherent value of individual contributions. This ongoing practice not only fortifies the fabric of familial relationships but also imbues the household with a sense of unity, a shared purpose, and a collective journey enriched by the threads of gratitude.

In the Smith household, a simple glass jar takes center stage in their family ritual. This "Gratitude Jar" serves as a daily reminder to appreciate life's blessings, big and small. Each family member, from parents to children, jots down one thing they're thankful for every day on a small slip of paper.

Come Sunday evening, the family gathers to read aloud the week's collection of gratitude's. This practice has not only strengthened their bonds but also cultivated a more positive home environment. The Smiths have found that regularly expressing thankfulness has shifted their focus from life's challenges to its joys, creating a warmer, more supportive family dynamic.

Reflection Questions:

1. Reflect on a recent instance where you expressed gratitude to a friend or family member. How did it impact your relationship?
2. How can you make gratitude a more consistent practice in your personal relationships?

Strengthening Bonds Through Thankfulness

Thankfulness transcends the boundaries of mere words; it serves as a cornerstone for fortifying trust in both the dynamics of business and personal relationships. Within the business sphere, a culture immersed in gratitude generates a profound effect, enhancing employee engagement and elevating job satisfaction to unprecedented heights. The simple act of expressing appreciation creates a ripple effect, prompting team members to channel their energy and enthusiasm wholeheartedly into their work, fostering an environment where each contribution is valued and acknowledged.

Gratitude is an art that deepens emotional connections in personal relationships. Within circles of friends and families, a shared commitment to acknowledging and appreciating each other's support, advice, and mere presence establishes an atmosphere rich in love and support. Gratitude emerges as a bridge that gracefully spans differences, fortifying bonds that withstand the test of time.

The act of expressing thankfulness becomes a symbolic reinforcement of the overarching ethos of the TRUST Principle. Leaders and individuals who embrace gratitude actively acknowledge the interconnectedness of trust, replication, utilization, and service, thus engaging in a deliberate practice. This acknowledgment, akin to the aforementioned well-orchestrated symphony, resonates with the cumulative impact these pillars have on cultivating robust relationships and steering endeavors toward success.

Example:

A monthly "Gratitude Day" has become a cherished tradition. On this day, employees take time to write heartfelt thankyou notes to colleagues who have helped or inspired them. This simple practice has had a profound impact, significantly improving workplace culture and fostering a strong sense of community. By encouraging regular expressions of appreciation, Acme has created an environment where employees feel valued and motivated, leading to increased job satisfaction and productivity.

Reflection Questions:

1. How does expressing gratitude in your workplace or personal life affect your relationships?
2. What are some practical ways you can express thankfulness more consistently?

The Gratitude Pillar A Tapestry of Appreciation in Business

In the intricate mosaic of business strategies, where profits and competition often share the spotlight, an often underestimated yet profoundly influential force quietly weaves its magic gratitude. This force, residing under the Gratitude pillar of the TRUST Principle, possesses the transformative power to turn transactions into relationships, clients into partners, and employees into devoted advocates. Let's embark on a journey through some of the most remarkable examples of gratitude in the business world, seamlessly interwoven with the essence of the TRUST Principle.

1. Zappos' Customer Delight:

Zappos, the online shoe and clothing retailer, has set a remarkable precedent for gratitude driven business practices. Their renowned customer service isn't a mere transactional exchange; it's an art form dedicated to going the extra mile. Zappos representatives are empowered to invest as much time as necessary to create a positive customer experience. This commitment to service aligns seamlessly with the Serve pillar of the TRUST Principle. By prioritizing customers' needs over rigid timelines, Zappos builds trust and loyalty that extends far beyond a single transaction.

2. Southwest Airlines' Employee Focus:

Southwest Airlines, celebrated for its exceptional customer service, profoundly understands the power of gratitude toward employees. The "Spirit Magazine" regularly features articles that showcase the accomplishments and significant milestones of their employees. This practice, aligned with the Thank pillar, cultivates an environment where employees don't just feel appreciated but are genuinely invested in the company's success. The motivated and highly valued workforce at Southwest Airlines is regarded as a crucial component in their commitment to achieving excellence.

3. Google's Innovation Days:

Google, the tech giant, spearheads "Innovation Days" where employees are encouraged to work on passion projects unrelated to their usual roles. This practice echoes the Replicate pillar, replicating the spirit of experimentation and innovation typically associated with smaller startups. Google fosters a culture of creativity and trust by granting employees the freedom to explore their ideas, which ultimately leads to groundbreaking discoveries and advancements.

4.   Amazon's Customer Centricity:

Amazon's unrivaled success is intricately tied to its customer centric approach. This alignment with the Trust pillar, specifically Replicate and Serve, is evident through Amazon's consistent focus on replicating successful strategies across markets and their relentless commitment to serving customer needs. Amazon establishes trust and brand loyalty that surpasses geographical borders by consistently improving the customer experience.

5.   Patagonia's Environmental Stewardship:

Patagonia, renowned for its outdoor apparel, doesn't merely produce quality products but embodies the Utilize and Serve pillars by aligning its business with environmental causes. The "Worn Wear" initiative encourages customers to repair and reuse their products, promoting sustainability. The strategic use of resources and unwavering commitment to a greater cause resonate with customers who share similar values, fostering a deeper sense of trust and loyalty.

6.   Microsoft's Inclusive Design:

Microsoft's inclusive design strategy, which focuses on creating products accessible to everyone, is a testament to the Utilize pillar. Microsoft's commitment to recognizing and harnessing the diverse talents and needs of their user base enables them to create products that cater to a wide range of individuals, fostering inclusivity and building trust in their brand.

Incorporating gratitude into business strategies aligns harmoniously with the principles of the TRUST Principle. These examples illustrate that gratitude isn't a fleeting sentiment; it's a strategic approach that radiates authenticity, sincerity, and commitment. As businesses incorporate gratitude into their core values, they pave the way for enduring relationships, empowered employees, and create a legacy built on trust.

Reflection Questions:

1. How can you incorporate gratitude into your business strategies to build stronger relationships and trust?
2. What are some examples of gratitude driven practices you can implement in your workplace?

Abraham Lincoln's Thanksgiving Proclamation Gratitude Amidst Adversity

In the crucible of the American Civil War's strife, President Abraham Lincoln wielded a proclamation that would etch Thanksgiving into the annals of national holidays. It was in the year 1863 when the nation, trapped in the clutches of conflict and turmoil, experienced a pivotal moment. Against this backdrop of adversity, Lincoln made a poignant choice—to express gratitude for the blessings that endured amid the chaos.

Lincoln's proclamation beckoned Americans to set aside a dedicated day for "Thanksgiving and Praise to our beneficent Father who dwelleth in the Heavens." As the war raged on, causing immeasurable loss of life and tearing families apart, Lincoln perceptively understood the critical importance of gratitude in revitalizing a common sense of purpose and shared principles.

This historical tableau serves as an interesting testament to the enduring power of thankfulness, even in the bleakest of times. Lincoln's proclamation transcended mere formality; it stood as an act of leadership, a call to unity and reflection. Through the expression of gratitude, Lincoln sought to nurture a collective sense of humanity and hope, impressing upon citizens the vital importance of acknowledging even the smallest blessings in the face of seemingly insurmountable adversity.

Reflection Questions:

1. How can you find and express gratitude even during challenging times?
2. What are some small blessings you can acknowledge and appreciate in your life?

The Ten Lepers Gratitude as a Transformative Act

Within the New Testament's sacred pages, the tale of the ten lepers unfolds as a poignant narrative, weaving a profound tapestry of the impact of gratitude. In this particular biblical account, there were ten individuals who were suffering from leprosy, a condition that caused them to be rejected by society. Despite their social isolation, they approached Jesus with a humble plea, seeking his divine intervention and healing. With great compassion, Jesus instructs them to go and show themselves to the priests, and as they embark on this journey, a miraculous healing takes place.

Notably, among the ten individuals who experienced this divine healing, only one decides to go back to Jesus. This lone figure, humbled and overwhelmed with gratitude, prostrates himself at Jesus' feet, offering heartfelt thanks. In response, Jesus expresses surprise and poses a poignant question, "Were not all ten cleansed? Where are the other nine?" He then imparts a profound insight into the grateful leper, asserting that his faith has not only led to physical healing but has also brought about holistic wellness.

This specific biblical parable serves as a powerful reminder of the immense power that is unleashed when we choose to express gratitude. Expressing gratitude goes beyond mere acknowledgment of received blessings, fostering a profound connection between the giver and the receiver. Jesus' recognition of the grateful leper's faith underscores the spiritual depth of gratitude as a conduit for healing and profound transformation.

The story of the ten lepers resounds throughout the ages, serving as a perpetual reminder that gratitude surpasses mere politeness. Through the genuine expression of gratitude, we not only show appreciation for the generosity of others but also nurture a spirit of humility, connection, and transformative grace.

Reflection Questions:

1.   Reflect on a time when expressing gratitude profoundly impacted your life or someone else's.
2.   How can you make gratitude a more integral part of your spiritual practice or daily routine?

As we delve into the Thank pillar, let us not forget that gratitude is not merely a sentiment; it is a potent practice that breathes life into relationships and acts as a catalyst for boosting morale. A simple expression of thanks, whether in the professional or personal sphere, contributes to an environment where trust not only thrives but also becomes the nourishing soil in which collaboration flourishes, and bonds strengthen. Through insightful real-life examples, let us peel back the layers of the Thank pillar, unveiling the transformative potential held within the humble phrase "thank you."

Reflection Questions

1. Reflect on a recent experience where you served others. How did it impact both you and the recipients of your service?
2. What steps can you take to make service a more integral part of your daily life?

The ability to establish, grow, extend, and restore trust is the key professional and personal competency of our time.

– Stephen M.R. Covey

7

TRUST IN ACTION

APPLYING THE TRUST PRINCIPLE EVERY DAY

Integrating the TRUST Principle into Daily Life

INTEGRATING THE TRUST Principle into our daily lives and embarking on this transformative journey necessitates the use of a guiding roadmap. The following is a comprehensive breakdown and guide, which highlights the conscious integration of the pillars of trust, replication, utilization, service, and gratitude into our daily actions.

Pillar Breakdown: Action Steps and Purpose

Pillar	Action Steps	Purpose
Trust	Delegate tasks and trust your team's capabilities.	Cultivate a culture of empowerment and collaboration.
	Communicate openly and honestly, fostering transparent relationships.	Build a foundation of trust among peers and colleagues.

Pillar	Action Steps	Purpose
Replication	Identify successful strategies and practices.	Ensure consistency and quality in your endeavors.
	Document procedures for future reference.	Save time and resources by replicating effective approaches.
Utilization	Recognize the strengths of individuals around you.	Create an environment where everyone can contribute fully.
	Delegate tasks that align with everyone's strengths.	Maximize efficiency and productivity within your team.
Service	Prioritize active listening in your interactions.	Show respect and empathy to foster meaningful connections.
	Offer assistance and support without hesitation.	Foster a culture of mutual aid and shared success.

Personal Transformation Through Daily Application

As you implement these practices, a profound shift will unfold within and around you. Trust will establish a strong foundation for your relationships, cultivating an environment that encourages authenticity and collaboration. Replication will allow you to consistently deliver excellent outcomes, establishing a reputation for reliability. Utilization will harness your team's collective strengths, igniting innovation and nurturing growth. Service will shape your daily interactions, leaving behind a trail of kindness and mutual support. Gratitude will fill each day with positivity, enhancing connections and uplifting morale.

It is essential to recognize that the TRUST Principle involves a gradual transformation, rather than a sudden overhaul. By effortlessly including these actions in your daytoday routine, you intertwine the threads of trust, replication, utilization, service, and gratitude into the very foundation of your life.

Cultivating Trust in Daily Interactions

Trust serves as the bedrock of any flourishing relationship, whether within the professional sphere, social circles, or family dynamics. Establishing trust demands active engagement and intentional commitment. Here's how you can nurture trust in your daytoday interactions:

1. Open and Transparent Communication:
    *   Forge trust through honesty in your communication. Ensure clarity, accuracy, and transparency. Avoid exaggeration and withholding information. Follow through on commitments to showcase reliability and appreciation for open dialogue.

2. Active Listening:
    *   Engage in genuine listening with others. Pay keen attention, pose followup questions, and display empathy. When individuals feel heard, they are more likely to trust your motives and reciprocate respect.

3. Consistency in Actions:
    *   Align your actions with your words over time. Predictability in behavior fosters a sense of security in interpersonal interactions.

4. Vulnerability and Authenticity:
    *   Embrace openness about your challenges and admit when uncertainty prevails. This vulnerability humanizes you and encourages others to reciprocate, deepening the bonds of trust.

5. Honoring Commitments:
    *   Uphold trust by delivering on your promises. Consistently meeting commitments communicates reliability and dedication to the relationship.

6. Avoiding Gossip and Negativity:

   • Steer clear of discussions involving speaking ill of others. Gossip corrodes trust and casts doubt on your intentions and loyalty. Focus on positive aspects and constructive discussions.

7. Respecting Boundaries:

   • Acknowledge personal and professional boundaries. Trust is dynamic, and honoring boundaries is crucial in cultivating that trust.

8. Empowering Others:

   • Demonstrate trust in your colleagues and friends by delegating tasks and responsibilities. This elevates their confidence and underscores your belief in their capabilities.

9. Acknowledging Mistakes:

   • Showcase humility and accountability by openly admitting mistakes. Taking responsibility and offering sincere apologies fortifies the trust others place in your character.

10. Valuing Feedback:

    • Welcome feedback from peers and incorporate it into your growth journey. Considering others' input shows that you value and respect their opinions.

Reflection Questions:

1. How can you improve transparency and openness in your communications?
2. What steps can you take to ensure consistency in your actions and words?

Practical Strategies for Replicating Success

The Replication pillar invites us to distill wisdom from our triumphs and integrate those lessons into our ongoing journey of growth. Here are pragmatic strategies to infuse the spirit of replication into your daily pursuits:

1. Identify Successful Patterns:
   - Delve into past successes and identify the strategies, approaches, or habits that played a key role in achieving positive results.

2. Document Best Practices:
   - Create a repository of best practices, documenting step-by-step procedures, decision-making frameworks, and pivotal insights.

3. Adapt, Don't Duplicate:
   - While the core idea remains steadfast, tailor strategies to align with the nuances of the current situation.

4. Focus on Core Principles:
   - Zoom in on the fundamental principles that underpinned a strategy's success, focusing on these when applying success to new contexts.

5. Train and Share Knowledge:
   - Empower your team by imparting training on successful strategies. Share the wisdom and understanding gained from past successes.

6. Encourage Experimentation:
   - Create an environment that promotes innovation and builds upon successful strategies, fostering a culture of creative evolution.

7. Monitor and Evaluate:
   - Regularly scrutinize the performance of replicated strategies. Conduct evaluations to gauge effectiveness and adjust course when necessary.

8. Feedback Loop:
   - Establish a robust feedback loop where team members share their experiences with replicated strategies.

9.   Celebrate Replication:

*   Cheer and honor successful replications, reinforcing the significance of seeking and implementing strategies that have proven effective.

10. Foster a Culture of Learning:

*   Cultivate an environment where learning from both successes and failures is cherished.

Reflection Questions:

1.   What successful strategies from your past can you replicate in your current projects?
2.   How can you adapt proven approaches to fit the unique needs of your current situation?

Utilization as a Daily Practice

The Utilization pillar calls for recognizing and amplifying individual strengths. Here's a strategic roadmap to infuse utilization into your daily interactions:

1.   Identify Strengths:

*   Observe the strengths, skills, and talents of those around you. Each person possesses something invaluable.

2.   Delegate Strategically:

*   Align tasks with the strengths of individuals, heightening their engagement and yielding superior outcomes.

3.   Empower Decision Making:

*   Trust team members by empowering them to make decisions within their areas of expertise.

4.   Encourage Skill Development:

*   Provide opportunities for individuals to hone their strengths.

5. Foster Collaborative Environments:

    •   Cultivate an atmosphere where team members feel at ease sharing their strengths and collaborating on projects.

6. Break Down Silos:

    •   Advocate for cross functional collaboration to promote effective teamwork and synergy.

7. Recognize Contributions:

    •   Publicly acknowledge and celebrate the distinctive contributions of team members.

8. Lead by Example:

    •   Exhibit your own strengths and encourage others to do the same.

9. Offer Mentorship:

    •   Pair team members with complementary skills for mentorship.

10. Adapt Roles:

    •   Exhibit flexibility by redefining roles to match changing strengths.

Reflection Questions:

1. How can you better recognize and utilize the strengths of those around you?
2. What steps can you take to encourage cross functional collaboration and skill sharing?

Acts of Service in Daily Life

The Serve pillar urges us to actively contribute to the growth and wellbeing of others. Here's a strategic guide to daily service practices:

1. Small Acts of Kindness:

    •   Engage in simple acts of kindness, such as holding the door open or offering a compliment.

2. Active Listening:

    •   Practice active listening by giving your full attention to the speaker.

3. Offer Assistance:

    •   Extend help without hesitation when you observe someone struggling with a task.

4. Share Knowledge:

    •   Share your expertise with those who can benefit.

5. Support in Challenges:

    •   Show support and stand alongside others during their challenging moments.

6. Volunteer Opportunities:

    •   Actively seek volunteer opportunities in your community or workplace.

7. Show Gratitude:

    •   Regularly acknowledge and thank others for their contributions.

8. Encourage Others:

    •   Empower and inspire others as they work towards their goals.

9. Collaborate Selflessly:

    •   Engage in collaborative efforts that prioritize the success of the team above personal benefits.

10. Acts of Generosity:

    •   Surprise someone with an occasional random act of generosity.

Reflection Questions:

1. Reflect on a recent experience where you served others. How did it impact both you and the recipients of your service?
2. What steps can you take to make service a more integral part of your daily life?

The Daily Practice of Thankfulness

Gratitude is a dynamic force that enriches your wellbeing and weaves threads of strength between you and those who share your journey. Making gratitude a part of your everyday routine can greatly change your relationships and your entire perspective on life. Here's a guide to cultivating thankfulness:

1. Morning Reflection:
    *   Begin each day by reflecting on things you're grateful for.
2. Express Appreciation:
    *   Nurture your relationships by expressing gratitude throughout the day.
3. Keep a Gratitude Journal:
    *   Record moments of gratitude in your journal, shaping your mindset into one that savors the good.
4. Practice Mindfulness:
    *   Navigate through your experiences with mindfulness, attuned to the blessings in your life.
5. Count Your Blessings:
    *   Regularly take stock of your blessings.
6. Thank Yourself:
    *   Embrace self-appreciation and thank yourself for your hard work and accomplishments.
7. Write Thank You Notes:
    *   Craft heartfelt thankyou notes, expressing sincere gratitude.
8. Gratitude Meditation:
    *   Visualize the things you're thankful for during meditation.
9. Reflect Before Sleep:
    *   Reflect on moments that brought you joy or made you thankful before going to sleep.

Any intelligent fool can make things bigger, more complex, and more violent. It takes a touch of genius — and a lot of courage to move in the opposite direction.

— E.F. Schumacher

CHAPTER 8

CHALLENGES TO THE SIMPLICITY OF THE TRUST PRINCIPLE

THE TRUST PRINCIPLE often gets overshadowed in a world obsessed with modernity and novelty. This chapter offers a detailed analysis of the formidable challenges that have gradually undermined these timeless principles over the past three decades. Join us on this enlightening journey as we peel back the layers of complexity and unravel the concealed beauty of the Trust Principle, examining the diverse factors—from the pervasive influence of a hyper focused and result driven culture to the revolutionary impact of the digital age—that have collectively veiled its true essence.

The Allure of Complexity

As the world has undergone transformative evolution, so too have our approaches to problem-solving. The pervasive belief that more intricate solutions inherently lead to superior outcomes often accompanies the pursuit of complexity. In this quest, however, there is a risk of veering away from the fundamental and simple tenets that underpin the core of the Trust Principle—trust, collaboration, and gratitude.

1. Illusion of Progress

    *   The allure of complexity can create a deceptive perception of progress. People commonly believe that if a process is complicated, it must be innovative and superior. However, this assumption doesn't always hold true; simplicity often paves the way for more efficient and effective outcomes.

2. Prestige and Ego

    *   In a competitive landscape, the temptation to showcase intellect and skills through complex solutions becomes pronounced. It becomes a matter of prestige and ego, with the misguided belief that complexity reflects competence. True mastery, however, lies in simplifying the complex.

3. Fear of Oversimplification

    *   There's a legitimate fear that simplification might lead to oversimplification, potentially leaving out crucial details. Yet, the art lies in distilling complex ideas into their essential components while retaining their integrity.

4. Desire for Uniqueness

    *   Many people find complexity appealing because it is associated with the longing for individuality. The aspiration is to stand out by presenting something intricate and novel. However, the true differentiator often lies in delivering clarity amidst complexity.

5. Overlooking Fundamentals

    *   In the relentless pursuit of complexity, fundamental principles might be overlooked. Sometimes, when individuals become too focused on crafting intricate strategies, they may unintentionally overlook the fundamental basics that are essential for achieving success.

6. Overestimating Sophistication

    *   It is common for individuals to overestimate the value of sophistication. Yet, the most impactful solutions are often the simplest. Complexity might impress momentarily, but simplicity endures.

7.   Compensating for Insecurity

  •   The allure of complexity can stem from a need to compensate for perceived inadequacies. The general belief is that by creating something intricate, one can effectively hide any vulnerabilities.

8.   Neglecting Communication

  •   Effective communication may face obstacles due to the complexity inherent in the process. Ideas become convoluted and conveying them to others becomes a challenge. Simplicity facilitates understanding and engagement.

9.   Overloaded Systems

  •   In business and technology, the drive for complexity can result in overloaded systems that are difficult to manage. The pursuit of simplicity in design can often contribute to smoother operation and maintenance.

10. Straying from Core Values

  •   Surrounded by complexity, there is a potential for losing focus on essential beliefs. Simplicity helps in staying connected to foundational principles and objectives.

While complexity may hold a certain allure, it's crucial to recognize that the pillars of the Trust Principle thrive in simplicity. Embracing trust, replication, utilization, service, and gratitude transcends the superficial glamor of intricacy, leading to a profound understanding of the foundational principles that foster efficiency, clarity, and lasting success.

The Influence of a Result Driven Culture

In the relentless pursuit of success, organizations often find themselves entangled in the pressures of a result driven culture. Although the attainment of tangible outcomes is undeniably crucial, it is important to bear in mind that this unwavering focus can unintentionally obscure the foundational principles embodied by the Trust Principle. Let's delve into the repercussions of a result driven culture and unravel why integrating trust, replication, utilization, service, and gratitude is not just beneficial, but essential.

1. Short Term Gains vs. Long Term Value
   - A culture fixated on results tends to prioritize immediate gains over long-term value. This myopic approach can lead to decisions that sacrifice trust and relationships in favor of fleeting successes.

2. Erosion of Trust
   - The trust between individuals diminishes when an excessive emphasis is placed on achieving outcomes. When outcomes take precedence without considering collaboration and open communication, trust within teams and with stakeholders gradually erodes.

3. Neglecting Process Improvement
   - A hyperfocus on results can divert attention from process improvement. Organizations run the risk of becoming complacent, thus failing to capitalize on opportunities to replicate and improve successful practices.

4. Underutilized Talent
   - In a resultdriven environment, talent may be underutilized. If individuals' strengths are not utilized to their full potential, it can hinder both personal growth and the productivity of the team.

5. Limited Adaptability
   - Adaptability may be compromised when an individual or organization adopts a result driven approach. Organizations might resist change or hesitate to explore alternative approaches due to the fear of deviating from established pathways.

6. Emotional Toll
   - Individuals in a result driven culture can experience burnout and stress because of the constant pressure to achieve

outcomes. The absence of service and gratitude exacerbates this toll on wellbeing.

7. Diminished Collaboration

    •   Collaboration tends to be neglected or not given its due importance in an environment that is primarily focused on achieving specific outcomes. People might find themselves in competition rather than cooperation, as the focus leans more toward individual achievements than collective success.

8. Fading Appreciation

    •   In the rush to meet targets, expressions of gratitude become scarce. This scarcity can lead to a demotivated workforce, as individuals may not feel adequately valued for their contributions.

9. Innovation Stagnation

    •   It is ironic that when individuals solely focus on achieving results, it can actually impede the process of innovation. Innovation demands a commitment to experimentation and a willingness to explore qualities that may be compromised within a rigid, results focused framework.

10. Shifting Paradigms

    •   Transitioning from a result driven culture to one rooted in the Trust Principle requires redefining success. It's about recognizing that trust, collaboration, and ethical conduct are integral to sustainable achievement.

Balancing a results driven culture with the Trust Principle involves finding a delicate harmony. While results remain essential, they must be achieved within a framework that values relationships, continuous learning, and a genuine appreciation for the contributions of all. The integration of trust, replication, utilization, service, and gratitude doesn't negate success; rather, it enhances it, rendering it enduring, meaningful, and holistic.

The Impact of the Digital Age

In the era of unprecedented technological advancements, the digital age has bestowed upon us both remarkable opportunities and challenges that intricately weave into the fabric of the Trust Principle. As we navigate a world characterized by swift technological evolution and seamless connectivity, it becomes crucial to delve into the impact of digital dynamics on the essential aspects of trust, replication, utilization, service, and gratitude.

1. Redefining Trust
   - In the digital landscape, trust takes on multifaceted dimensions. It extends beyond face-to-face interactions to encompass the security of data, the reliability of technology, and the authenticity of online relationships. The importance lies in striking a balance between this new dimension of trust and its traditional counterpart.

2. Virtual Replication
   - Digital platforms enable the global replication of content and ideas. However, the challenge lies in ensuring the authenticity and integrity of replicated information amidst an era dominated by misinformation.

3. Utilization in a Remote World
   - The realm of remote work and virtual collaboration necessitates innovative utilization of skills. Leaders must effectively recognize strengths, even in virtual settings, and harness them adeptly.

4. Digital Service Dynamics
   - Online support and virtual assistance are key components of the service's digital transformation. The challenge is to create genuine, empathetic interactions within the confines of the digital interface.

5. Gratitude in Virtual Interactions
   - Expressing gratitude through digital channels might lack the emotional impact of in person interactions. One of the key

aspects of navigating this challenge is to discover methods of expressing genuine gratitude while operating within the limitations of the online environment.

6. Erosion of Human Connection

    - Although digital connectivity has the potential to erode genuine human connection, it also enhances communication. Striking a delicate balance between the efficiency of digital interactions and the emotional richness of face-to-face encounters is crucial.

7. Amplified Complexity

    - Digital systems can introduce complexity, leading to intricate processes that might overshadow the simplicity of the Trust Principle. In order to stay competitive in the digital age, it becomes absolutely essential to strive for streamlined digital solutions.

8. Data Ethics and Trust

    - Given the dominance of data in today's era, it becomes crucial to prioritize ethical data handling as a means to maintain trust. Upholding data privacy and security seamlessly aligns with the principle of trust.

9. Adaptation and Learning

    - The digital age demands continuous adaptation and learning. Individuals and organizations must replicate successful digital strategies while staying open to innovative approaches.

10. Rekindling Humanity

    - Amidst the digital transformations, the Trust Principle stands as a poignant reminder to rekindle the essence of humanity. Balancing technology with authentic human connection ensures a harmonious digital era.

The ability to navigate the complexities of the digital age requires individuals to purposefully and seamlessly integrate the foundational elements of the Trust Principle into the rapidly changing digital environment. The rapid pace of change doesn't diminish their relevance;

rather it magnifies it. We can ensure that technology doesn't overshadow the foundations of human relationships and success by infusing trust, replication, utilization, service, and gratitude into digital interactions.

Navigating Competitive Mindsets

In the realm of innovation and growth, competitive mindsets create a symphony of ideas, driving individuals and organizations towards progress. However, this drive, if unchecked, can construct barriers that jeopardize collaboration and undermine the very foundations of the Trust Principle. Mastering the art of cultivating a culture of healthy competition while upholding trust, replication, utilization, service, and gratitude demands a nuanced approach. Here's a guide on how to navigate the terrain of competitive mindsets adeptly.

1. Collaboration Over Isolation

   • Instead of isolating to protect ideas, embrace collaboration. Engage with others to share insights and cocreate solutions that mutually benefit everyone involved.

2. Fostering Mutual Growth

   • Shift the focus from outdoing others to fostering mutual growth. When the collective aim is to elevate everyone, an environment conducive to collective success naturally emerges.

3. Emphasizing Common Goals

   • Highlight common goals that unite individuals and teams. When everyone rallies around shared objectives, competition becomes a means to achieve those collective aspirations.

4. Recognizing Unique Contributions

   • Celebrate individual strengths and contributions without diminishing others. Acknowledge that everyone brings something distinctive and valuable to the collaborative table.

5. Encouraging Ethical Behavior

    •   Encourage ethical conduct, even when faced with intense competition. Upholding integrity and fairness builds trust and prevents harmful rivalry.

6. Transforming Failures into Learning Opportunities

    •   Embrace failure as an important opportunity for profound learning, rather than fearing it. A competitive mindset, when coupled with a growthoriented perspective, thrives on resilience and continuous improvement.

7. Nurturing Ecosystems, Not Silos

    •   Encourage the development of ecosystems that facilitate crossfunctional collaboration. Break down silos and foster an environment where diverse skills converge, enriching the collective dynamic.

8. Constructive Feedback Culture

    •   Embrace feedback for positive development. The establishment of a culture that encourages constructive criticism has the potential to empower individuals and teams, allowing them to enhance their approaches and ultimately benefiting the entire collective.

9. Celebrating Collective Success

    •   Rejoice in both individual achievements and collective victories. This practice reinforces the notion that success is not a solitary pursuit but is enhanced and sustained when shared.

10. Balancing Personal Growth with Team Success

    •   Strive for personal growth while considering how it aligns with team success. Balancing personal aspirations with collective objectives maintains a cooperative atmosphere where individual and team achievements coalesce seamlessly.

The process of navigating competitive mindsets does not revolve around the elimination of competition. It's about infusing it with the principles of trust, replication, utilization, service, and gratitude. When competition is viewed as a dynamic catalyst for growth and collaboration, it strengthens relationships and propels individuals and teams toward shared success.

Short-Term Thinking and its Effects

In the whirlwind of short-term thinking, where immediate gains can dazzle and captivate, there lies a subtle erosion of the very principles encapsulated in the Trust Principle. A focus on quick wins that never wavers, while providing a fleeting sense of triumph, has the potential to silently undermine trust, obstruct the replication of successful strategies, overlook the effective utilization of resources, dilute service quality, and mute expressions of gratitude. Let's embark on a journey into the nuanced effects of short-term thinking and unravel why embracing the vista of the long term is not just prudent but imperative.

1. Trust Erosion

    • The pursuit of short-term gains can inadvertently sow the seeds of distrust. Decisions geared solely toward immediate outcomes may sideline the concerns of teams and stakeholders, eroding trust.

2. Hindrance to Replication

    • Short-term thinking often casts a shadow over the replication of successful practices. Instead of embracing and duplicating effective strategies, the focus remains myopically fixed on the allure of immediate results.

3. Underutilized Resources

    • A myopic mindset neglects the rich potential of resources. Opportunities to optimize skills and assets for long-term gains are overlooked, leading to the underutilization of valuable resources.

4. Diminished Service Quality

    • The relentless pursuit of quick outcomes may sacrifice service quality. In the race for short-term profits, the nurturing of customer relationships might take a back seat, resulting in a decline in service standards.

5. Lack of Gratitude

   • In the haste for short-term victories, the importance of gratitude often fades into the background. Teams might bypass the moments of appreciation, inadvertently contributing to decreased morale.

6. Missed Innovation

   • Short-term thinking creates a stifling environment for innovative thinking. The relentless focus on existing solutions leaves little room for the exploration of new and potentially more effective approaches.

7. Ignored Long-Term Consequences

   • Decisions guided by short-term thinking may neglect to acknowledge the profound long-term implications. Neglecting the future impact of choices made today can pave the way for unforeseen challenges down the road.

8. Reduced Adaptability

   • The champions who embrace a long-term perspective are those who prioritize adaptability in the face of changing circumstances. Conversely, short-term thinking breeds rigidity, fostering a resistance to change.

9. Dimmed Sustainability

   • The relentless pursuit of immediate gains often overshadows sustainability. Short-term triumphs overshadow long-term planning and responsible resource management.

10. Missed Opportunities for Growth

   • A fixation on short-term goals can inadvertently hinder personal and organizational growth. Embracing the long-term perspective opens doors for continuous improvement and expansion.

Embracing the long-term perspective is not a dismissal of short-term achievements. It's a delicate dance that strives for equilibrium, holding dear the principles of trust, replication, utilization, service, and gratitude. Individuals and organizations can achieve lasting success by looking beyond short-term gains and focusing on timeless values.

Traditional Hierarchies and Trust

In organizational dynamics, traditional hierarchical structures have been the goto, providing clear authority lines but creating obstacles for open communication and collaboration. Let's unravel the nuances of the impact traditional hierarchies wield on trust and delve into strategies to traverse them effectively.

1. Power Imbalance and Trust

    *   Traditional hierarchies often carry the weight of power imbalances, casting shadows on the landscape of trust. The fear of consequences can lead subordinates to refrain from expressing concerns or innovative ideas.

2. Hindered Open Communication

    *   The presence of rigid tiers within traditional hierarchies can create obstacles that hinder open communication. Information may be confined to specific echelons, stifling the free flow of ideas and impeding transparency.

3. Limited Autonomy and Innovation

    *   Autonomy and innovation often face limitations within hierarchical systems as they tend to impose restrictions and hinder progress. Team members may feel constrained, unable to make decisions that transcend the confines of their designated roles.

4. Challenge to Utilization

    *   The structured nature of hierarchies may impede the effective utilization of skills. Valuable talents could go unnoticed if they don't neatly align with the hierarchical blueprint.

5. Barrier to Service

    •   A rigid hierarchy can stand as a formidable barrier to the spirit of service. The emphasis on structure might overshadow the innate willingness to serve others within the organization.

6. Trust Through Empowerment

    •   The delicate art of balancing hierarchy and trust involves the empowerment of individuals at all levels. Trust naturally flourishes when team members are empowered to contribute, irrespective of their position in the hierarchy.

7. Encouraging Cross Level Communication

    •   Promote the crosspollination of ideas through communication across different hierarchical levels. Breaking down these barriers fosters an environment where diverse perspectives can intermingle.

8. Building Trustworthy Leadership

    •   Trustworthiness is a crucial quality that leaders within a hierarchy must embody. Their actions and decisions set the tone for trust dynamics within the organization, influencing how others perceive and reciprocate trust.

9. Fostering Collaborative Culture

    •   Cultivate a collaborative culture that places value on contributions from all levels. The adoption of this approach effectively mitigates the negative impacts of hierarchy, leading to an environment that cultivates collaboration.

10. Recognizing Contributions

    •   Acknowledge and celebrate the contributions of individuals regardless of their hierarchical position. This practice instills a sense of value and recognition throughout the organization.

Effectively navigating the labyrinth of traditional hierarchies demands a delicate balance between structure and flexibility. The Trust Principle can not only coexist within hierarchical structures but also flourish when leaders prioritize building trust, fostering open communication, and recognizing the unique strengths of individuals. The integration of hierarchy and trust allows organizations to cultivate a balanced and collaborative workplace.

Revisiting Management Practices

In the ever-evolving landscape of management, where practices adapt to the shifting currents of business dynamics, the Trust Principle emerges as a guiding light, unveiling opportunities to transform workplaces into realms of effectiveness, harmony, and sustainability. Here's an interesting exploration of how you can synchronize management practices with the pillars of trust, replication, utilization, service, and gratitude.

1. Trust Centric Leadership
   - Embrace a trust centric leadership paradigm as a transition from the traditional command and control model. Empower teams with autonomy, champion open communication, and cultivate an environment where psychological safety flourishes.

2. Replication as Knowledge Sharing
   - Redefine knowledge sharing practices. Encourage teams to be generous with successful strategies, fostering a culture where continuous improvement is a shared endeavor.

3. Adaptive Utilization
   - Reimagine the utilization of skills. Move beyond rigid roles and embrace a model that emphasizes harnessing individual strengths while providing avenues for continuous growth and skill enhancement.

4. Servant Leadership
   - Embrace the principles of leading by serving. Prioritize the needs of your team members, offering the support and resources necessary for their individual and collective flourishing.

5. Cultivating Gratitude
   - Infuse gratitude into the fabric of management practices. Regularly recognize and appreciate the efforts of your team, crafting a positive atmosphere that serves as a catalyst for sustained motivation.

6. Employee Centric Approach

    •   Shift from a purely outcome driven mindset to one that prioritizes the wellbeing, growth, and development of individual team members. Consider these factors as integral elements of success.

7. Feedback and Development

    •   Make feedback a continuous and constructive practice. Provide insights that facilitate both personal and professional growth, thereby enhancing overall team performance.

8. Collaborative Decision Making

    •   Emphasize the importance of collaborative decision-making. Improved outcomes and a sense of ownership and collective responsibility are both benefits of involving team members.

9. Agile and Adaptable

    •   Adopt agile management practices that facilitate quick adaptation. This ensures the organization remains responsive and resilient in the face of evolving environments.

10. Balanced Metrics

    •   Strive for a balanced approach to metrics of success. Evaluate team and individual performance by incorporating both short-term achievements and long-term value creation.

When you reframe management practices through the prism of the Trust Principle, you're not only optimizing business operations, but also transforming the way your organization operates. Embracing contemporary leadership involves aligning management practices with foundational principles, weaving a tapestry of success that is not only holistic but sustainable.

Socioeconomic Changes and Trust

The intricate dance of socioeconomic shifts, propelled by technological marvels, developing demographics, and dynamic consumer behaviors, intricately weaves the tapestry of trust in novel ways.

Navigating this intricate terrain, all while upholding the fundamental tenets of the Trust Principle, demands a keen adaptability and a nuanced comprehension of the emergent dynamics at play. Here's an insightful exploration into how socioeconomic changes influence trust, as well as how to deftly navigate this evolving landscape.

1. Digital Trust
    *   Trust takes on a new form in this digital age. Cybersecurity, data privacy, and the delicate art of managing one's online reputation emerge as pivotal factors in constructing digital trust.

2. Multigenerational Workforce
    *   The shifting demographic landscape brings forth a diverse tapestry of generations in the workforce. Building trust now involves a nuanced understanding of and response to the unique values and needs of each generation.

3. Remote Work Culture
    *   The surge in remote work necessitates a recalibration of trust dynamics. Transparent performance measurement, effective communication tools, and ensuring remote team members feel acknowledged and valued become the cornerstones of trust.

4. Cultural Diversity
    *   With increased cultural diversity, the demand for cultural intelligence surges. Trust is enhanced through the embrace and respect of diverse perspectives and backgrounds.

5. Changing Consumer Behavior
    *   The importance of consistent quality and transparent communication in building trust is elevated by evolving consumer behaviors, which are shaped by unprecedented access to information.

6. Gig Economy Dynamics
    *   The gig economy introduces a fresh interplay of trust between organizations and freelancers. Trust grows when

everyone is compensated fairly, expectations are clear, and communication is open.

7. Sustainability and Ethical Practices

- Socioeconomic changes underline the significance of sustainability and ethics. Trust is established when organizations visibly prioritize ethical practices and environmental responsibility.

8. Mental Health Awareness

- Mental health awareness is highlighting the importance of trustbased leadership. Creating a workplace characterized by psychological safety and unwavering support becomes paramount.

9. Flexibility and Adaptation

- The ever-shifting socioeconomic landscape demands leaders who embody flexibility and adaptability. Trust flourishes when decisionmakers pivot gracefully, embracing change and prioritizing the wellbeing of their teams.

10. Data Ethics and Transparency

- Data ethics and transparency are closely intertwined with trust, as data plays a central role in shaping this connection. Organizations that handle data responsibly and openly communicate their practices cultivate a foundation of trust.

In this intricate dance with socioeconomic changes, the key lies in a commitment to staying informed, embracing diversity, and fostering a culture of continuous learning and adaptation. Through the integration of the Trust Principle in this dynamic environment, individuals and organizations not only adapt to change but also proactively foster trust in a continuously evolving world.

In this world, there was nothing scarier than trusting someone. But there was also nothing more rewarding.

— Brad Meltzer

CHAPTER 9

EMBRACING SIMPLICITY
REINVIGORATING THE TRUST PRINCIPLE

Prioritizing Relationships Over Results

IN A WORLD driven by tangible outcomes, the idea of prioritizing relationships may appear paradoxical. However, this chapter explores how prioritizing relationships enriches the Trust Principle and leads to sustainable success. Relationships are the lifeblood of any organization or personal endeavor. When we focus on building and nurturing relationships, we create an environment where trust can flourish. This approach may seem counterintuitive in a results-oriented culture, but it is relationships that ultimately drive sustainable success. Prioritizing relationships fosters collaboration, mutual respect, and a sense of belonging, all of which are crucial for long-term achievement. By investing in relationships, we ensure that trust, loyalty, and a shared vision become the foundation of our endeavors, leading to outcomes that are not only successful but also meaningful and enduring.

1. Nurturing Trust through Relationships

    -   Making relationships a priority creates fertile ground for trust to grow. When individuals sense genuine value and respect, trust becomes an organic byproduct, laying a robust foundation for enduring success.

2. Collaboration Over Competition

    -   A focus on relationships fosters collaboration over competition. Teams that value interpersonal success over individual achievements collaborate more seamlessly, unlocking collective potential.

3. Sustainable Growth through Relationships

    -   Relationships fuel sustainable growth. Organizations that prioritize relationships construct enduring networks that contribute to long-term success.

4. Collective Learning and Adaptation

    -   Prioritizing relationships encourages collective learning. Teams engaged in open communication learn from each other's experiences, paving the way for adaptable strategies.

5. Resilience in Challenges

    -   Resilience is fostered through strong relationships. Teams fortified by robust relationships support one another, navigating challenges with collective strength.

6. Authentic Service through Relationships

    -   Relationships enhance authentic service. Deep-rooted connections lead to meaningful and sincere commitment to others' wellbeing.

7. Appreciation and Gratitude

    -   Valuing relationships encourages gratitude. Recognizing unique contributions fosters an atmosphere of appreciation and shared success.

8. Emotional Intelligence and Empathy

    -   Relationships elevate emotional intelligence and empathy. Leaders who prioritize relationships develop deep rapport with their teams, creating a workplace infused with emotional intelligence.

9. Balanced Well Being

    • Prioritizing relationships promotes balanced wellbeing. When individuals feel connected and supported, their overall wellbeing thrives.

10. Legacy of Meaningful Impact

    • Prioritizing relationships leads to a legacy of meaningful impact. Positive relationships and lasting contributions define true success, going beyond temporary outcomes.

Rediscovering the Power of Simplicity

Rediscovering simplicity involves a conscious effort to remove unnecessary layers and focus on what truly matters. It is about distilling complex ideas into their most effective and impactful forms. This process requires a deliberate approach to identify the core principles that drive success and to strip away extraneous details that may cloud our judgment or hinder our progress. Simplicity does not mean oversimplification; it means refining our focus to enhance clarity and efficiency. By concentrating on the essential elements, we can make more informed decisions, improve communication, and foster an environment where innovation and collaboration can thrive. Simplicity empowers us to see the bigger picture and align our actions with our most important goals.

1. Clear Foundations of Trust

    • Free from convoluted processes and hidden agendas, trust flourishes in an environment of straightforwardness, honesty, and reliability. By eliminating unnecessary complexity, we create a clear path for building and maintaining trust.

2. Amplifying Replication Efforts

    • Simplicity amplifies the effectiveness of replication efforts by ensuring that successful strategies are easily understood and implemented. Distilling these strategies to their core elements allows for seamless adoption and adaptation across various contexts, enhancing consistency and performance.

3. Unveiling Individual Potential

    - Simplified roles and tasks allow individual talents to shine. When people are not bogged down by unnecessary complexities, they can focus on their strengths and make meaningful contributions. This clarity in roles enhances engagement and maximizes the potential of each team member.

4. Service in its Purest Form

    - Simplicity revitalizes service by focusing on genuine engagement and value delivery. By removing unnecessary steps and barriers, service interactions become more effective and meaningful. This approach ensures that the needs of service recipients are met with sincerity and efficiency.

5. Essence of Gratitude

    - Simplicity magnifies the essence of gratitude by highlighting the importance of small, everyday acts. Recognizing and appreciating these simple gestures fosters a culture of mutual respect and thankfulness, which strengthens relationships and builds a positive organizational culture.

6. Decisive and Informed Choices

    - Simplified decision-making processes lead to more decisive and informed choices. By presenting information clearly and concisely, we facilitate better understanding and quicker decisions. This efficiency enhances trust and ensures that decisions are made with confidence and clarity.

7. Transparent and Effective Communication

    - Simplicity elevates communication by removing jargon and ensuring messages are clear and direct. Transparent communication builds trust and fosters meaningful connections, making it easier for teams to work together effectively and harmoniously.

8. Adaptable Agility
    *   Simplicity fuels adaptability by focusing on essential principles and flexible strategies. A simplified framework allows organizations to pivot quickly in response to changes, ensuring they remain resilient and effective in dynamic environments.

9. Growth Guided by Clarity
    *   Simplicity guides personal growth by providing clear and achievable goals. When individuals have a clear understanding of their objectives, they can navigate their developmental journeys with confidence and purpose, fostering continuous improvement and self-trust.

10. Bridging Differences with Ease
    *   Simplicity bridges differences by emphasizing shared values and common goals. By focusing on these foundational principles, organizations can create unity and harmony amidst diversity, ensuring that all voices are heard and respected.

The Power of Simplicity

Embracing simplicity is not about disregarding complexity but rather about understanding and managing it. By focusing on the essential, we can enhance the impact of each pillar of the Trust Principle. Simplicity allows us to cut through the noise and concentrate on what truly matters, facilitating clearer communication, more efficient processes, and stronger relationships. It helps us to identify and focus on core values and principles, which in turn fosters an environment where trust, collaboration, and gratitude can thrive. By simplifying our approach, we make it easier to replicate successful strategies, utilize individual strengths, and provide genuine service. This focus on simplicity ultimately leads to more meaningful and sustainable outcomes, both in our professional and personal lives.

1. Trust in Clear Intentions
    *   Trust thrives on transparency and clear intentions. Simplicity aids in the direct communication of goals and

values, minimizing the potential for misunderstandings. By keeping intentions straightforward, we ensure that trust is built on a solid foundation of mutual understanding and clear expectations.

2. Replication Without Complication

   • Successful strategies can be lost in translation when they are overly complicated. Simplicity in replication ensures that the core principles of effective practices are maintained. By keeping replication straightforward, teams can more easily adopt and adapt these practices, fostering consistency and reliability across the organization.

3. Efficient Utilization of Strengths

   • The identification and utilization of individual strengths become more manageable when roles and tasks are simplified. Simplicity allows individuals to focus on what they do best, leading to higher productivity and job satisfaction. Streamlined roles enable team members to contribute effectively, enhancing overall team performance.

4. Service Through Genuine Engagement

   • Service excellence is rooted in understanding and meeting needs genuinely. Simplicity in service interactions removes unnecessary barriers, allowing service providers to focus on delivering authentic value. When interactions are straightforward, both service providers and recipients benefit from a more meaningful and effective exchange.

5. Gratitude in the Everyday

   • Simplicity brings attention to the small, everyday gestures that make a significant impact. By appreciating the simple contributions and acts of kindness, we foster a culture of gratitude that permeates all levels of an organization. This ongoing recognition of small efforts can significantly boost morale and create a positive environment.

6. Streamlined Decision Making

    *   Decision making can often be bogged down by unnecessary complexity. Simplicity streamlines this process, ensuring that decisions are made efficiently and inclusively. Clear decision-making protocols build trust as they demonstrate a commitment to transparency and fairness, ensuring that all voices are heard.

7. Transparent Communication

    *   In an age of information overload, simplicity in communication is crucial. Clear and concise communication helps to eliminate misunderstandings and ensures that messages are effectively conveyed. This transparency builds trust and fosters stronger, more meaningful connections between individuals and teams.

8. Agile Adaptation

    *   Simplicity aids in agility, allowing organizations to respond swiftly to change. By focusing on core principles and avoiding unnecessary complications, organizations can pivot more effectively in dynamic environments. Simplified strategies facilitate quick adaptation, ensuring resilience and sustained success.

9. Personal Growth Through Clarity

    *   Simplicity offers clarity in personal and professional development goals. Clear, straightforward objectives enable individuals to chart their growth paths effectively. This clarity fosters confidence and trust in their abilities, leading to more focused and purposeful development.

10. Harmony in Diversity

    *   Simplicity fosters harmony by emphasizing shared values and common goals. In diverse environments, focusing on these foundational principles helps bridge differences and create a unified, cohesive community. Simplifying the approach to diversity ensures that all perspectives are valued and integrated seamlessly.

Embracing simplicity is a transformative force that strips away unnecessary complexities, revealing the timeless principles encapsulated within the Trust Principle. By prioritizing relationships, individuals and organizations can create environments where trust, replication, utilization, service, and gratitude naturally flourish. This shift not only leads to authentic relationships and effective strategies but also paves the way for enduring success in a complex world.

Trust should be a quality that you constantly work to perfect within yourself. Otherwise, what legacy are you leaving for the next generation?

– John Fleck

CHAPTER 10

THE ENDURING LEGACY OF THE TRUST PRINCIPLE

THE ECHO OF the Trust Principle reverberates through the corridors of time, casting its influence for both the present and the unfolding future. This chapter thoroughly examines the enduring impact of the core principles—trust, replication, utilization, service, and gratitude—culminating in a legacy that remains steadfast despite the relentless passage of time. Here's a nuanced exploration into the timeless legacy of the Trust Principle.

Passing Down Trust through Generations

The Trust Principle metamorphoses into a legacy when trust becomes an ancestral bequest. Leaders who champion trust instill a legacy steeped in integrity and authenticity, inspiring successive generations to cherish and uphold these bedrock values. This transfer of trust shapes cultures and environments where integrity is valued, leading to sustainable success and strong, reliable relationships.

Ever Relevant Replication

Strategies that withstand the test of time become everlasting wisdom. Each generation refines and adapts these strategies, ensuring their relevance in the ever evolving landscapes of change. The process of replication allows for the preservation of proven methods while incorporating new insights and innovations, creating a continuous cycle of improvement and adaptation.

Harnessing Ancestral Skills

The Trust Principle promotes the strategic application of ancestral skills. Preserving priceless abilities by incorporating old wisdom into modern situations protects them from being eroded by the unrelenting passage of time. This approach ensures that valuable knowledge and skills are not lost but are utilized to address contemporary challenges effectively.

Servant Leadership's Ripple Effect

A legacy of service spawns a ripple effect that transcends generations. Leaders prioritizing service sow seeds of positive impact, leaving an indelible mark that extends far beyond the immediate successors. Servant leadership creates environments where the wellbeing and development of others are paramount, fostering a culture of mutual support and collective growth.

Gratitude's Generational Resonance

Gratitude reverberates across generations. Leaders nurturing a culture of gratitude sow seeds for an enduring appreciation, fostering a legacy that endures the trials of time. By consistently expressing gratitude, leaders build strong, resilient communities where individuals feel valued and motivated to contribute their best.

Guiding the Ethical Path

The Trust Principle evolves into an unwavering moral compass. Organizations and individuals guided by these principles craft ethical legacies, providing a steadfast framework for future decisions and actions. Ethical behavior becomes ingrained, ensuring that integrity and trustworthiness are maintained in all endeavors.

Trust Amid Technological Shifts

The enduring legacy of the Trust Principle seamlessly adapts to technological shifts. Even as tools advance, the unwavering principles of trust continue to keep individuals and organizations grounded in the everchanging world of technology. By prioritizing trust, organizations can navigate technological advancements without losing sight of core values.

Lessons in Adaptation

Generational leaders deftly navigate change, guided by adaptive principles. The Trust Principle imparts the art of embracing change without compromising on core values, fostering resilience. This ability to adapt while staying true to foundational principles ensures sustained success in dynamic environments.

Reflecting the Human Spirit

The Trust Principle reflects the unyielding essence of the human spirit. It stands as a testament to humanity's intrinsic yearning for connection, growth, and meaningful contributions that transcend the temporal constraints of boundaries. By embracing these principles, individuals and organizations can create a legacy that resonates with the fundamental aspects of human nature.

A Beacon in Uncertain Times

In times of uncertainty, the Trust Principle stands unwavering as a beacon. Its timeless principles provide solace and guidance, serving as a stable anchor in turbulent and rapidly changing environments. The Trust Principle offers a sense of stability and direction, helping individuals and organizations navigate challenges with confidence and integrity.

Reclaiming the Trust Principle A Continuum of Transformation

Our odyssey through the realms of trust, replication, utilization, service, and gratitude has brought us full circle, unveiling these pillars not as disparate principles but as interconnected threads of transformation. Together, they orchestrate growth, resilience, and positive metamorphosis.

As we venture beyond the confines of these pages, let's carry the Trust Principle as a reference. Let's infuse its simplicity into our interactions, decisions, and aspirations. In doing so, we become stewards of an enduring legacy—a legacy that nurtures trust, catalyzes growth, and enriches lives. Each trust laden action, replicated success, and act of service brings us closer to a world where the Trust Principle is an involuntary response in our lives.

As we conclude this chapter, it is evident that the Trust Principle is not merely a set of guidelines but a profound legacy that transcends time. The enduring impact of trust, replication, utilization, service, and gratitude weaves a tapestry that connects past wisdom with future potential.

The Lasting Influence of Trust

Trust remains the cornerstone, passed down through generations, fostering environments where integrity and authenticity thrive. It is the bedrock upon which all meaningful relationships and successful endeavors are built.

Replication and Continuity

Replication ensures that effective strategies and practices are preserved and adapted, allowing for continuous improvement and sustained success. This principle guarantees that the wisdom of today becomes the foundation for the achievements of tomorrow.

Utilization of Timeless Skills

The strategic use of ancestral skills highlights the importance of integrating historical knowledge with modern innovation. This blend of old and new equips individuals and organizations to navigate contemporary challenges with a strong, informed foundation.

The Ripple Effect of Service

Service, as a guiding principle, creates a ripple effect that extends far beyond immediate actions. It fosters a culture of support, kindness, and positive impact that transcends generations, leaving a lasting mark on society.

Gratitude's Resonance

Gratitude, woven into the fabric of daily interactions, nurtures an environment of appreciation and mutual respect. It is a powerful force that enhances morale, strengthens bonds, and promotes a culture of positivity that endures through time.

A Moral Compass

The Trust Principle serves as an ethical guide, ensuring that decisions and actions align with core values. This moral compass is vital in navigating the complexities of the modern world while maintaining a commitment to integrity and ethical behavior.

Adapting to Change

As technology and societal norms evolve, the Trust Principle adapts, providing stability and guidance. It ensures that even in a rapidly changing environment, the core values of trust, replication, utilization, service, and gratitude remain relevant and impactful.

The Human Spirit

Ultimately, the Trust Principle reflects the indomitable human spirit. It embodies the essence of connection, growth, and meaningful contributions, transcending temporal constraints and fostering a sense of belonging and purpose.

Looking Ahead

As we move forward, let us embrace the Trust Principle not just as a framework but as a way of life. By integrating these timeless values into our daily actions and decisions, we create a legacy that nurtures trust, catalyzes growth, and enriches lives. Each act of trust, every replicated success, and every genuine service brings us closer to a world where the Trust Principle is an instinctive part of our existence, guiding us toward a brighter, more connected future.

He who sweats more in training bleeds less in battle.

– George S Patton, Jr

CHAPTER 11

NURTURING EXCELLENCE THROUGH CONTINUOUS TRAINING (BONUS)

WITHIN THE EVERCHANGING context of the Trust Principle, training emerges as a crucial and dynamic element. Far from a static event, training embodies an intrinsic and perpetual process resonating not only within corporate corridors but also echoing in the personal nooks of our lives. The significance of continuous training is surveyed in this chapter, emphasizing its pivotal role in shaping business interactions and fostering personal growth.

The Interview Process: The First Step in Training

Amidst intricate business dynamics, the pillar of training reveals itself as a foundational thread woven seamlessly from the very inception, starting with the pivotal interview process. Yet it's crucial to view this stage as more than a routine evaluation; it's a gateway to cultivating profound trust by aligning expectations seamlessly.

A perceptive interviewer acknowledges the great power of asking precisely tailored questions. These questions transcend mere interaction; they are the very building blocks of trust construction. By crafting queries that delve into the company's ethos, aspirations, and the essence of the Trust Principle, an interviewer offers the candidate a tantalizing preview of the organizational culture they might inhabit. This glimpse goes beyond surface impressions; it delves deep into the core values and principles forming the bedrock of the company's existence.

The significance of a well-structured interview process reverberates across the candidate's experience. It transforms the interview room into a microcosm of trust cultivation. A prospective employee encountering an interviewer diligently upholding the values of the Trust Principle feels assured that their potential workplace values trust, collaboration, and authenticity.

On the other hand, a laissez-faire approach to interviews can set off a chain reaction of consequences. The lack of careful consideration may lead to dissonance between the company's actual culture and the expectations of the new hire. This discord can ultimately cascade into high turnover rates and a disjointed work environment where the promise of trust remains unfulfilled.

Evolving Beyond Formative Stages: A Culture of Continuous Learning

While formal training programs undeniably play a crucial role in fostering trust within a team, their impact reaches new heights when harmonized with the philosophy of continuous learning. A team, akin to any living organism, demands regular nurturing and refinement to reach its optimal thriving state.

Scheduled training sessions serve as crucibles where team members are not just equipped with tools and insights but are also empowered to replicate successes, enhance stakeholder service, and genuinely embody gratitude. This isn't a mere routine exercise; it's a dynamic conduit through which the Trust Principle surges, saturating the team environment with cohesion, vibrancy, and resilience.

The spectrum of training sessions spans from structured leadership workshops to experiential teambuilding exercises. These engagements provide platforms for both individual growth and the cultivation of collective strengths. The results of these efforts are palpable—a team that flawlessly reproduces effective strategies, serves clients with unwavering dedication, and fosters an atmosphere of trust and collaboration.

In this context, training evolves from an obligatory process into a profound culture that continually refines and amplifies the Trust Principle. It's an acknowledgment that trust is not static; it requires constant nurturing and recalibration to remain vibrant and effective. By embracing this philosophy, businesses create an environment where the Trust Principle flourishes, enhancing both individual development and collective success.

Training Beyond Business: A Lifelong Journey

In the wide scope of learning, stretching far beyond formal settings like offices and desks, it is an ongoing influence that intertwines with every aspect of our daily lives. The Trust Principle and its pillars aren't singular events but an ongoing commitment to personal and collective evolution. Much like Chick-fila maintains its service standards universally, we too replicate these principles across diverse domains.

This commitment to replication extends into our personal growth journey, a relentless pursuit of knowledge and transformative experiences. Similar to Starbucks replicating its ethos worldwide, we infuse our principles with innovative vitality through seminars, discussions, and books. With each endeavor, we replicate our dedication to continuous improvement, perpetuating the Trust Principle through our actions.

Reflection Questions

Congratulations on completing this chapter! Reflecting on what you've learned is an essential step towards integrating these principles into your daily life. To help you process and apply these concepts, I've provided a series of reflection questions.

Personal Trust Development:

- How has continuous training impacted your personal growth?
- Can you recall a situation where additional training helped rebuild trust in a professional setting?

Types of Trust:

- In your current personal and professional relationships, which type of trust (interpersonal, organizational, societal) do you find most challenging to maintain through continuous training? Why?
- Identify an organization you trust deeply. What specific training practices have contributed to this trust?

Building and Maintaining Trust:

- Reflect on a time when continuous learning played a crucial role in building trust. How did it impact your relationship with your team or colleagues?
- Think about a promise you kept recently that was related to your professional development. How did fulfilling this commitment strengthen your relationship with the other person?

Expert Insights:

- Which expert insight on continuous training and trust resonated most with you? How can you apply this insight to improve trust in your personal or professional life?
- How does vulnerability in acknowledging the need for continuous learning influence your ability to build trust? Can you think of a time when showing this vulnerability helped you connect more deeply with someone?

Practical Strategies:

- Of the practical strategies listed (transparency, keeping promises, showing vulnerability, active listening, expressing gratitude, building consistency, encouraging collaboration, providing support), which do you find easiest to implement in continuous training? Which do you find most challenging and why?

- Choose one practical strategy that you haven't focused on much. Develop a plan to incorporate this strategy into your continuous learning interactions over the next month. What specific actions will you take?

Intersections of Trust:

- How do you see the different types of trust (interpersonal, organizational, societal) intersecting in your life through continuous training? Provide an example where trust in one area influenced trust in another.
- Reflect on a time when a breach of trust in one area of your life affected your willingness to engage in continuous training. What lessons did you learn from this experience?

Real-life Applications:

- After reading about Johnathan Reyes and Horizon Enterprises, identify a similar reallife example from your own experience or observation. How did continuous training play a role in their success?
- How can you apply the lessons from Horizon Enterprises to your own life or organization? What steps can you take to replicate their approach to continuous learning and trust building?

Reflecting on these questions will deepen your grasp of trust and help you craft a tailored plan to strengthen it in your relationships. Your "Trust Notebook" serves as a personal space for ongoing reflection and growth, becoming an invaluable asset in your journey to build stronger, more trusting connections.

APPENDIX FURTHER READING AND RESOURCES

IF YOU'VE FOUND value in exploring the TRUST Principle and wish to delve deeper into similar concepts and ideas, the following books and resources might be of interest to you. These works, like the TRUST Principle, offer insights into personal growth, building relationships, and thriving in various aspects of life.

1. "The 7 Habits of Highly Effective People" by Stephen R. Covey

Covey's timeless principles guide readers toward personal effectiveness and meaningful relationships. Similar to the TRUST Principle, this book emphasizes core values, trust-building, and continuous improvement.

2. "Daring Greatly" by Brené Brown

Brené Brown's work explores vulnerability, courage, and connection. Just as the TRUST Principle emphasizes the importance of authenticity and vulnerability, Brown's insights encourage us to embrace these qualities for deeper connections.

3. "Start with Why" by Simon Sinek

Simon Sinek's book examines the power of purpose and motivation. Aligning with the TRUST Principle, Sinek's work emphasizes the significance of understanding "why" in our actions, fostering trust and meaningful engagement.

4. "The Power of Now" by Eckhart Tolle

This book delves into the philosophy of mindfulness and being present. Similar to the TRUST Principle's focus on simplicity and authenticity, Tolle's teachings guide us toward a more fulfilled and present life.

5. "Drive The Surprising Truth About What Motivates Us" by Daniel H. Pink

Pink's exploration of motivation and human behavior aligns with the TRUST Principle's emphasis on recognizing strengths and understanding what drives individuals and teams.

ONLINE RESOURCES

1. OpenAI's GPT-3 Resources

Explore OpenAI's resources on personal development, effective communication, and relationship-building to deepen your understanding of the principles explored in the TRUST Principle.

2. TED Talks

TED Talks offer a plethora of talks on trust, personal growth, and collaboration. Search for topics related to trust-building, authenticity, and effective communication to expand your knowledge.

3. LinkedIn Learning

LinkedIn Learning provides courses on leadership, communication, and personal development. These courses can complement your journey of applying the TRUST Principle in various aspects of your life.

Remember that the pursuit of personal growth and meaningful relationships is a continuous journey. These resources, much like the TRUST Principle, serve as guides to help you navigate this journey with wisdom, purpose, and authenticity

ABOUT THE AUTHOR

BORN AND RAISED in West Virginia, John Fleck is a seasoned leader and researcher with 25 years dedicated to studying and practically applying servant leadership. Certified and mentored by John Maxwell and having served within the management team at Chick-Fil-A, he brings a wealth of leadership expertise to every venue. Passionate about creating positive change both locally and globally, his book, "The TRUST Principle," is a testament to the enduring values instilled in him by the good people of "The Mountain State" as well as all of the people that have touched his life in a beautifully positive way. A true advocate for leadership with integrity, John infuses timeless principles into his daily tasks and encounters, offering a roadmap for success and authenticity in the modern world. To contact John W Fleck visit JWFLECK.com.

www.ingramcontent.com/pod-product-compliance
Lightning Source LLC
Chambersburg PA
CBHW022058020426
42335CB00012B/733